Your Faithful Brain: Designed for So Much More!

Leonard Matheson

WESTBOW
PRESS
A DIVISION OF THOMAS NELSON
& ZONDERVAN

Copyright © 2014 Leonard Matheson.

All rights reserved. No part of this book may be used or reproduced by any means, graphic, electronic, or mechanical, including photocopying, recording, taping or by any information storage retrieval system without the written permission of the publisher except in the case of brief quotations embodied in critical articles and reviews.

Scripture taken from the Holy Bible, NEW INTERNATIONAL VERSION®. Copyright © 1973, 1978, 1984 by Biblica, Inc. All rights reserved worldwide. Used by permission. NEW INTERNATIONAL VERSION® and NIV® are registered trademarks of Biblica, Inc. Use of either trademark for the offering of goods or services requires the prior written consent of Biblica US, Inc.

WestBow Press books may be ordered through booksellers or by contacting:

WestBow Press
A Division of Thomas Nelson & Zondervan
1663 Liberty Drive
Bloomington, IN 47403
www.westbowpress.com
1 (866) 928-1240

Because of the dynamic nature of the Internet, any web addresses or links contained in this book may have changed since publication and may no longer be valid. The views expressed in this work are solely those of the author and do not necessarily reflect the views of the publisher, and the publisher hereby disclaims any responsibility for them.

ISBN: 978-1-4908-5857-9 (sc)
ISBN: 978-1-4908-5858-6 (hc)
ISBN: 978-1-4908-5859-3 (e)

Library of Congress Control Number: 2014919541

Printed in the United States of America.

WestBow Press rev. date: 11/21/2014

Contents

Dedication xi
Preface xiii
A Note about References and Resources xv

Chapter 1: Your Brain Is Designed for Redemption
 and Rehabilitation 1
 "... *Rehabilitate* the World through Him"? 1
 Hoodlum in the Music Room 2
 Rancho's God Connection 5
 Peter Grows Up 7
 A Prodigal Son 8
 What's the Focus of *Your Faithful Brain?* 11
 Chapter Takeaways 13
 Discussion Questions 14

Chapter 2: The Faithful Brain of Jesus 15
 "Jesus grew ..." 16
 Can We Really Study the Brain of Jesus? 17
 So My Brain Is Just Like Jesus' Brain? 19
 How Can Jesus Guide Me? 25
 Why Should We Follow Jesus' Example? 26
 Chapter Takeaways 29
 Discussion Questions 29

Chapter 3: A Faithful Brain Is God-Integrated 30
 Ripples of Sin 30
 What's the Bottom Line? 32

What's a Faithful Brain?...................................34
How Does a Faithful Brain Develop?..............35
How Do I Interfere with Faithful Brain
    Integration?...37
How Did You Help Carol?...............................41
Brain Restorative Sleep..................................43
Personal Prayer Relaxation............................43
Goaling..44
Happy Hippocampus Exercise.......................45
Why Must I Start with God?...........................48
Chapter Takeaways...49
Discussion Questions.....................................50

Chapter 4: A Faithful Brain Is Relational........................51
"I Can't Stop Thinking about It!"....................52
How Does John 1:1 Guide Faithful
    Brain Development?....................................57
How Does Emotional Salience Pertain
    to the Bible?...60
How Can I Experience the Bible?...................63
How Did You Help Charlie?............................65
Chapter Takeaways...71
Discussion Questions.....................................72

Chapter 5: A Faithful Brain Is God-Rehabilitated............73
What Is a God-Rehabilitated Brain?...............74
Who Was the First Brain Injury Patient?.........76
When Did the Idea of Neuroplasticity Arise?....80
How Did Neurorehabilitation Develop?...........84
Should the Bible Inform Science?...................86
Chapter Takeaways...89
Discussion Questions......................................89

Chapter 6: A Faithful Brain Is Heart Balanced 90
    Does My Heart Think? 90
    "Nobody believes me! I'm not faking!" 91
    How Had Judy Gotten So Badly
        out of Balance? 93
    How Does My Heart Help My Brain Think? 99
    How Does Love Affect the Vagus Nerve? 102
    Why Are We Designed This Way? 103
    What Happened to Judy? 106
    Chapter Takeaways 109
    Discussion Questions 109

Chapter 7: A Faithful Brain Is Loving 110
    "You're not being fair!" 111
    What Is "New Covenant Love"? 112
    Is Marriage Necessary? 114
    Can I Learn New Covenant Love outside
        Marriage? 116
    What's the Neuroscience of Love? 119
    What Are Oxytocin and Cortisol? 120
    How Does Love Restore My Brain? 122
    How Does Marriage Affect My Health? 124
    Are There Many New Covenant Marriages? ... 126
    How Does Loving God Promote My Health? ... 128
    Chapter Takeaways 133
    Discussion Questions 133

Chapter 8: A Faithful Brain Is Grace-Blessed 134
    What Is Grace? 135
    Why Are Corrective Emotions Necessary? 137
    How Does God's Grace Help Me? 139
    What if I Don't Experience Corrective
        Emotions? 142

  Where Does Grace Show Up in the Brain?..... 144
  Chapter Takeaways... 148
  Discussion Questions 149

Chapter 9: A Faithful Brain Is Truth-Guided 150
  Whose Truth Is It? 150
  How Did You Embrace God's Truth?............... 153
  How Are Jesus' Way and Truth and
    Life Linked?... 156
  Where Do We Find God-Reflecting Virtues?... 158
  How Does Character Affect Us?..................... 160
  Chapter Takeaways... 161
  Discussion Questions 162

Chapter 10: A Faithful Brain Is Organized by God......... 163
  Why Are Cognitive Efficiency and Brain
    Organization Important? 164
  Why Is Values Confusion So Important? 167
  Why Are Jesus' Values So Important? 170
  How Can I Know I'm Following Jesus?........... 171
  How Can I Get Started? 172
  Chapter Takeaways... 175
  Discussion Questions 175

Chapter 11: A Faithful Brain Is Intentional 176
  "... a living sacrifice,
    holy and pleasing to God"? 177
  What Do You Want Most out of Life?............. 178
  What Is Joy?... 180
  How Can I Find Joy in Difficult
    Circumstances?.. 182
  How Did Danny Teach You about Joy? 186

Why Was Danny's Dependence on
    God Important?... 187
How Did the Bible Help You?......................... 191
Chapter Takeaways... 193
Discussion Questions 194

Glossary of Key Terms 195
Acknowledgments 207
References 209
Index 251

Dedication

This book is dedicated to Greg Holder, lead pastor at The Crossing in Chesterfield, Missouri. Greg has been my friend and spiritual mentor for most of my faith journey and has taught me and so many others about the critical importance of a relationship with Jesus. Guiding our growing and sometimes rambunctious community of seekers and believers, Greg has appealed to my spiritual and scientific curiosity and stimulated the intellectual exploration of our faith, which was the trigger for this book. Faith and neuroscience aren't normally considered compatible or even related to each other, but thanks to Greg, my experience has been quite different.

"Ask the big questions of our Faith. Ask the questions of life. Ask about what it is that matters most and see if there aren't answers. There is an intellectual honesty to Christianity. God says, 'Seek, ask, you'll find me.'" (Greg Holder, 2012)

Preface

Severely traumatized people have taught me that, through his design of our brain God makes life to the full possible in spite of our circumstances. The biblical narrative of redemption is intertwined with the human brain's transformative capacities. Recent neuroscientific evidence indicates that God designed our brains to participate in this opportunity, which I encourage people to take advantage of by developing "faithful brains". When we do so, we experience hope, joy, and peace, and we grow beyond our circumstances.

Faith and neuroscience usually are not considered in the same book, but they should be. My academic and professional training as well as my clinical experiences have led me to the inescapable conclusion that neuroscience is a modern opportunity to explore and deepen our faith in God.

The intersection of faith and neuroscience is controversial, but I hope we can examine it thoughtfully. I want *Your Faithful Brain* to encourage discussions about how faith and neuroscience are complementary. Please join the conversation in the Faithful Brain community on Facebook. We look forward to meeting you.

—Leonard N. Matheson, PhD, Faithful Brain Institute

A Note about References and Resources

Consilience is the process of bringing together evidence from apparently unrelated sources to create powerful new ideas. This book explores the consilience of faith and neuroscience; it is focused on the idea that the human brain was designed to function best within God's created reality.

If there's a God who created us for a personal relationship, the design of our brain should reflect this intention. To some, this is a powerful, old idea to which their beliefs led years ago. To others, this is an absurd idea; they believe that faith and neuroscience are incompatible.

To encourage exploration of this idea, I selected key *New International Version Bible* passages and then culled through thousands of neuroscientific studies to select a few hundred pertinent references from well-recognized scientists and scholars. Most of the studies in the Reference section are no more than a few years old. Neuroscience is developing so rapidly that studies and texts prior to the twenty-first century are included only if they're very highly regarded classics. All the references are from scientists and other thought-leaders to whom you should be introduced. The papers I selected are readily available and full of fascinating information. You can access these through Google Scholar or PubMed, where you can set up a free account to save your favorites. If you have additional references that may be helpful, please let me know.

If you're reading *Your Faithful Brain* as a self-development study, the Faithful Brain Fitness Challenge provides an analysis and recommendations for exploration and growth. For more information, go to faithfulbrainfitness.com, where you will also find free educational videos.

CHAPTER 1

Your Brain Is Designed for Redemption and Rehabilitation

> For God so loved the world that he gave his one and only son, so that whoever believes in him would not perish, but have eternal life. For God did not send his Son into the world to condemn it, but to "rehabilitate" the world through him.
> —*John 3:16–17*

Brain Basics

1. Your brain was designed by God to be redeemed and rehabilitated.
2. Your choice to trust God and follow Jesus optimizes your neurorehabilitation.
3. Your brain becomes ready for rehabilitation as you seek God's perfect will for your life.

"... *Rehabilitate* the World through Him"?

Did I startle you by substituting "rehabilitate" for "save" in the Scripture above? I made the switch to describe my life with Jesus; I am a broken man who was saved and is being rehabilitated.

I am a psychologist who practices neurorehabilitation. I help people put their lives back together after brain injuries, strokes, spinal cord injuries, or serious neurological diseases.

I believe we all need neurorehabilitation because only one of us has ever developed perfectly. I also believe the best way to practice neurorehabilitation is to combine neuroscience and faith in God. This seems to some people to be a mismatch, but it's not; they fit together very well.

I believe that God designed your brain to be ready for rehabilitation and sent Jesus to provide the necessary guidance. The "neuron heart" on the cover of this book represents how your brain responds to God's love, which triggers several neurorehabilitation processes. These processes operate as if God designed your brain to be rehabilitated by the lessons and example of Jesus.

And here's the most exciting part: no matter how old you are and no matter what you've done or what's been done to you, your brain can always be rehabilitated. It's never too late for redemption and rehabilitation.

Hoodlum in the Music Room

Peter[1] was big for a fifteen-year-old. He cursed and shouted profanities as Mrs. G. and I pushed him, wearing a safety helmet and strapped to his wheelchair, out of Ward 904 to the music room for our first counseling session.

Peter was one of my patients at Rancho Los Amigos National Rehabilitation Center in Downey, California. His abusive language upset most of the nurses and doctors, but

---

[1] The case studies describe real people. I use pseudonyms for my clients' names, and key facts have been changed to maintain their anonymity.

I had grown up on the streets and playgrounds of South Central Los Angeles, and Mrs. G. was from another planet.

A few weeks before, Peter had been stabbed in his head during a gang fight. The knife had pierced the right side of his skull and seriously damaged his brain. Peter had lost many of his normal inhibitions as well as the ability to use much of the left side of his body.

In the community hospital before coming to Rancho, Peter's arms and legs had been tied to his bed with "soft restraints" after he had regained consciousness. He was combative and threatened the staff. However, in the Pediatrics Pavilion at Rancho, restraints were not acceptable to Mrs. G. and to Dr. Elizabeth Eberle, the head nurse and pediatrician for teenagers with brain injuries. Children, even those who were violent, were encouraged rather than restrained. But Peter challenged those values.

Peter had come to Rancho the afternoon before, accompanied by his mother and grandmother, who obviously loved him in spite of his unceasing verbal abuse. Anticipating the fear that Peter's behavior would create, they had pleaded with us to give their boy a chance. But after praying at his bedside as he fell asleep that night, they had gone home sad and discouraged.

Fast-forward twenty-seven years. I am testifying before the United States Congress about rehabilitation. "Peter went on to live the American dream," I tell the assembled representatives. "He got a job, married, and became a father. He lives with his family in Southern California."

But that morning, when I was left alone with Peter in the music room, I didn't know our brain had been designed to prepare us for redemption. That first day with Peter, I accidentally tapped into Peter's God-designed brain, and though my efforts were very clumsy, I started on a journey that continues today.

After Mrs. G. left us, I had only a vague idea of what to do. Basically, my goal was to get Peter to stop his cursing so he wouldn't disrupt the staff and the five other boys with brain injuries who shared his room. We had only a few days to change his abusive behavior; the other patients had the right to not be frightened by what appeared to be a dangerous hoodlum.

The music room was soundproofed, but Peter's angry cursing was reverberating down Rancho's halls as I sat down and turned his wheelchair to face me. As I always do when I may be struck, I took off my eyeglasses. I spoke quietly to Peter, who continued shouting angry curses. I tried to soothe and calm him, but my words had absolutely no effect.

Fortunately, the music room was well lighted, and I noticed the telltale nicotine stain on the index finger of Peter's still-useful right hand. I said quietly, "Would you like a smoke?"

Whoa! Peter looked at me and stopped shouting. "Whattt?" he slurred. "Whuddd you say?"

I had his attention. "You can earn a smoke if you do what I say." I laid out nuts, bolts, and washers for a simple assembly task on the table. I put a washer on a bolt and twisted on a nut. There were enough parts for thirty assemblies. "Peter, each one of these you assemble earns you a penny, and you can buy a smoke for thirty cents."

Bam! Peter slammed his right arm on the table, scattering parts all over and started shouting again, even louder than before, with violent shaking and tears of desperate anger. He reached up, yanked his helmet off, and threw it at me.

I ducked, collected my wits, and picked Peter's helmet up. I held it in my lap as I continued to talk quietly to him.

"Peter, you know cigarettes aren't allowed in the hospital." More violent and belligerent cursing. "Well Peter, I can get a cigarette in here this evening if you want, but they cost thirty cents. You can earn thirty cents by putting these together."

Quiet. Wheels obviously turning. One loud exclamatory curse! Quiet once again. "O-o-o-o-k," he stuttered and settled back into his wheelchair.

"Good, Peter. Now help me pick up these parts. We have enough only for thirty, and you need thirty cents to buy a cigarette."

We spent the next three hours while Peter assembled the three simple parts, earning one penny for each assembly. Peter struggled with his one good hand, receiving less help from me as we went along. Peter was painfully clumsy and easily frustrated, and he stopped several times, but he always came back to the task, and he improved as he went along.

Peter completed the thirty sets just before we broke for lunch. I told Peter, "I have something that's more difficult. It has five parts, but it pays three cents for each set. Would you like to try that tomorrow? If you can handle it, you might be able to buy more smokes."

I can still remember his first smile and grunted chuckle more than forty-four years later. That was the beginning of Peter's rehabilitation that led him to a new life, transformed into a responsible young man his mother, grandmother, and friends barely recognized.

Rancho's God Connection

Early in his neurorehabilitation, Peter began asking, "Why did this happen? If there is a God, why did he let this happen?" He asked the question often in frustration and despair. I didn't have an answer for him, so I asked our hospital chaplain, Father Robert Gipson, to talk with Peter.

Father Bob was the priest in the small Catholic chapel at Rancho, the 210-acre rehabilitation hospital of the Los Angeles County University of Southern California Medical School. He spent most of his time visiting with the 1,200 inpatients and their families. In his sandals and black clerical shirt and slacks, he offered a calming presence as he worked with us to help turn tragedy into hope.

I noticed that Father Bob didn't argue with Peter and defend God; he listened quietly and affirmed the pain of Peter's trauma. By respectfully listening to his question and affirming his pain and anger, Father Bob gently guided Peter out of his gloom.

Gradually, Peter's question to Father Bob changed from angrily blaming God to "What am I supposed to do now?" Father Bob's answer was the same for Peter as it was for the hundreds of people we worked with together over the next several years: "God wants you to do your best, and he'll do the rest."

This is a simple but very deep answer. It includes both our responsibility and God's dominion. God is in charge, but we must trust and surrender.

"God wants you to do your best and he'll do the rest." Neuroscience now confirms that this is a great combination for neurorehabilitation, as if our brain was designed for Father Bob's answer. As I counseled Peter and his family alongside Father Bob, I began to see how faith and neuroscience complement each other.

Christians are fond of saying that "God is love" (1 John 4:8), but most nonscientists don't know the powerful impact of this idea on the human brain. Similarly, neuroscientists only recently have begun to understand the love-related brain rehabilitation processes to which we find references in Scripture written more than 2,000 years ago. In this book, I will describe a few hundred of the thousands of scientific studies that point to how embracing the idea that "God is love" promotes brain development and rehabilitation. Time and again, the scientific references and biblical references amplify understanding of each other. For me, this is very exciting!

Peter Grows Up

Even though Peter's brain had been seriously damaged, its built-in rehabilitation capacities provided him with a second chance at life. As Peter gradually accepted Father Bob's answer, his anxiety and anger lessened and he began to develop calm hope. This is the hope that protects the brain and heart and the rest of the nervous system so that neurorehabilitation can unfold.

As we watched Peter progress through his neurorehabilitation program, we saw a young man who still could be terrifying but whose behavior gradually softened. He began to respect authority and to develop character. He became cooperative and settled into work with the Rancho team on his goals. We began with Peter's goal to earn enough money for one cigarette and progressed through hundreds of small and large goals. Several hours each day, five days a week Peter pursued his goals in occupational therapy, speech therapy, physical therapy, and he attended the Rancho school.

As with any teenager, Peter's early goals were self-centered, and we accepted those as the means to an end. But even in his early, turbulent life, Peter had picked up important virtues and family values reinforced by his Catholic Church boyhood.

Eventually, Peter's goals began to reflect social and interpersonal values such as helping financially support his mother and grandmother. We helped Peter develop a list of goals that were linked to these values—walking with a brace, finishing high school, getting a job, and learning to drive a car with special controls. Every task in therapy and school was linked to these goals so that each held inherent meaning. Peter was exercising not only to comply with his therapist; he also pushed himself so he could eventually help his mother pay her rent.

As spring gave way to summer, Peter went home to live with his mother and grandmother. Rather than fall back in with his gang, he returned to high school as a sophomore. With the help of his family and teachers, he eventually graduated. He worked during school vacations at a furniture paint shop, cleaning up and doing work that developed his confidence.

After his graduation from high school, I worked with Peter's employer to rig up an electrostatic paint booth to allow him to work as a one-handed spray painter. If you have ever used a Steelcase desk, it might have been painted by Peter.

I lost track of Peter many years ago, but his story has continued to affect me. I introduced this chapter by writing, "No matter how old you are and no matter what you've done or what's been done to you, your brain can always be rehabilitated. It's never too late for redemption and rehabilitation." You should know something about me before we go any further.

A Prodigal Son

I began my career in neurorehabilitation as an antitheist. Like Jesus's parable of the prodigal son in the Bible (Luke 15:11–32), I had turned away from God. In the parable, one willful son cashed out his inheritance early and left his father, older brother, and family. He wasted his fortune a long way from home, was starving, and yearned to eat the food he had to feed pigs as a hired hand. In desperation, he headed home, convinced he was no longer worthy of his father's love.

But this is where Jesus surprised his audience. "While he was a long way off, his father saw him and was filled with compassion for him; he ran to his son, threw his arms around him and kissed him." He clothed his deeply apologetic son in the finest robe, placed a valuable ring on his finger, and arranged a lavish feast to celebrate his return. The older brother protested and did not join in the celebration, so his father pleaded with him, "My son, you are always with me and everything I have is yours. We must celebrate and be glad, because your brother was dead and is alive again; he was lost and now is found!"[1]

Although I had been raised in a loving Christian family, believed in God as a child and adolescent, and had married my Sunday school sweetheart, in early adulthood I became angry with God, rejected him, and went my own way. Initially, that was very liberating; I had Sundays free in Southern California! I could stretch Saturday night into a thirty-six-hour party, which is what I did. I got divorced and jumped into the Southern California lifestyle with abandon. Drinking and partying became my new gods.

After several years, however, I hit a hard bottom. I had driven my family and friends away. I felt lost, lonely, and empty of hope.

I didn't share the faith of Peter and Father Bob, but my experiences with them and many other clients started me to reconsider. I began to read the Bible from a scientist's perspective, starting with the first chapter of the gospel of John. It was tough going, and I stopped and started often. But I began to notice that there were several key passages in the Bible that aligned perfectly with neuroscience, some of the most important of which I look forward to sharing with you.

My transformation from anti-theist to Jesus-follower was strongly influenced by my growing knowledge of neuroscience. I was amazed that what I had learned in graduate school and in my career as a psychologist seemed to fit with what I was finding in the Bible. At first, I tried to ignore the connection, but it gradually became an undeniable fact, and then it became an undeniable experience.

As my study of neuroscience and Scripture progressed, I started to notice how their integration played out in my life. I began to recognize the wisdom available in the Bible and how both the Bible and neuroscience pointed to the importance of a relationship with Jesus. Rather than trying to reconcile bits and pieces of science and Scripture, I began to understand that participating in God's created reality was wholesome, beautiful, and growth producing.

On August 3, 1995, I was ready to commit my life to Jesus and start each day doing my best to pay attention and fit into God's plan. For several years up to that day, my prayers had been attempts to negotiate with God; that was my misunderstanding. Much of my prayer that day was beyond words; I confessed the mess I had made by keeping God at arm's length. My life seemed like a newsreel of guilt, embarrassment, and shame that I wanted to burn. I asked for forgiveness and invited Jesus to be my Lord and Savior. I told my wife and children and asked them to help me. I was baptized at Saddleback Church in Orange County, California a few months later.

Now, the consilience of neuroscience and faith encourages and excites me as I experience its benefits, compelling me to share my story. I hope you also will be encouraged and excited as you learn how God designed your brain to be ready for redemption and rehabilitation.

What's the Focus of *Your Faithful Brain?*

"What we commonly call the mind is a set of operations carried out in the brain."[2] page 5) Your brain, inextricably linked to your mind, is designed so you can experience what Jesus promised in John 10:10: "I have come that they may have life, and have it to the full." This is the life of loving sacrifice and trust that harnesses your brain's rehabilitative capacities. These capacities provide the resilience that a life of faith produces.

"Redemption and rehabilitation" are the focus of this chapter because I believe we need both, which was certainly true for me. Redemption is the instantaneous shift from one path to another that God provides when we accept Jesus as our Lord and Savior. Rehabilitation is what begins to happen to our brain as we walk down that path. By honestly examining my life and the lives of thousands of other Peters, I now appreciate my need for both.

It's important to understand that we often make choices that don't fit with our brain's design, what my Pastor Greg Holder[2] says "are less than God's best." As we do this, we interfere with optimal brain development, akin to a concussion interfering with normal brain processes. And if we persist with these choices, we create dedicated neural networks in

---

[2] Lead pastor, The Crossing, Chesterfield, Missouri.

the brain that make it more likely for future choices to further limit our growth.

Although we've all made harmful choices and we've all been hurt by the choices of other imperfect people, I believe we were designed for wonderful lives if we follow Jesus and implement God's design of our brain. We can help do this by paying close attention to the brain of Jesus. Rehabilitating our brain by following Jesus and studying his lessons develops neural networks that show up in our values and character and promote brain health and fitness.

It seems like rehabilitation is to the brain what renewal is to the mind; both lead to transformation that refers to the whole person. From my perspective, this is what the apostle Paul was encouraging us to do in Romans 12:2: "Do not conform to the pattern of this world, but be transformed by the renewing of your mind. Then you will be able to test and approve what God's will is—his good, pleasing and perfect will."[1]

For many years, the truth of Father Bob's answer to Peter just didn't make sense to me. In the linear brain of my young adulthood, which was hobbled by pride, cultural logic and values, the ideas of free will and surrendering to God were juxtaposed and mutually exclusive. I sought happiness, wealth, and fame without God, and I was successful at it for several years. I needed to test the boundaries of culturally defined freedom to discover its emptiness. And I got my just rewards; after I achieved cultural success beyond my wildest dreams, depression led me to suicidal futility.

With the help of several loving people, pastors, and friends, I was brought back to a relationship with God and began to develop a *faithful brain* integrated with God, within itself, and with others, and operating consistent with its design.

In a faithful brain, pride is replaced by humility and logic is balanced by wisdom and love. In a faithful brain, my daily choosing to surrender to God's trustworthy love made sense.

As Christian philosopher Dallas Willard wrote, "The ultimate freedom we have as human beings is the power to select what we will allow or require our minds to dwell upon ... We still have the ability and responsibility to try to retain God in our knowledge."[3] page 95) He explained that God would "make himself known to us" when we make the effort. If we can accept God as responsible for creation, our surrender to God will provide guidance that helps life expand without culturally determined limits. We flourish as we move in synchrony with God's created reality.

Redemption and rehabilitation are intertwined opportunities because "God so loved the world that he gave his one and only son." The same brain-restorative capacities that we helped Peter harness are available to us all, and I look forward to sharing them with you. To assist your faithful brain development, we have an assessment that will analyze your current status and provide you with a confidential report. You can participate in the Faithful Brain Fitness Challenge and obtain your report by going to www.faithfulbrainfitness.com. If you're reading *Your Faithful Brain* as a self-improvement study, I recommend that you do this before you read further; the report has several suggestions you will find useful.

Chapter Takeaways

1. Your brain was designed by God to be ready for redemption and rehabilitation.
2. The choice to trust God and follow Jesus triggers redemption and begins neurorehabilitation.

3. Emotions, thoughts, and behaviors are represented in the brain by neural networks.
4. Your choices affect your brain's development.
5. If you choose to surrender and seek God's perfect will for your life, powerful processes take place in the brain that optimize its design.

Discussion Questions

1. Are you excited or upset about the idea that neuroscience aligns with Scripture?
2. What do you think about the idea that your choices impact your brain's development?
3. Do any aspects of the stories of Peter or Len resonate with you and your story? In what ways?
4. What do you think the connections are among the way God designed your brain, being created in his image, and Jesus' promise of life to the full?
5. In the Faithful Brain Fitness Assessment, how did you feel about comparing your character to the character of Jesus?

CHAPTER 2

The Faithful Brain of Jesus

Every year, Jesus's parents went to Jerusalem for the Festival of the Passover. When he was twelve years old, they went up to the festival. After the festival was over, while his parents were returning home, Jesus stayed behind. Thinking he was in their company, they traveled on without him for a day. When they did not find him, they went back to Jerusalem to look for him. After three days they found him in the temple courts, sitting among the teachers, listening to them and asking them questions. Everyone who heard him was amazed at his understanding and his answers. When his parents saw him, they were astonished. His mother said to him, "Son, why have you treated us like this? Your father and I have been anxiously searching for you." "Why were you searching for me?" he asked. "Didn't you know I had to be in my Father's house?" But they did not understand what he was saying to them. Then Jesus went down to Nazareth with them and was obedient. His mother treasured all these things in her heart. And Jesus grew in wisdom and stature, and in favor with God and man.

—*Luke 2:41–52*

Brain Basics

1. All the brain's biological processes are affected by our experiences and behavior.
2. Neuroplasticity, neurogenesis, and neural epigenesis are ongoing processes that Jesus perfectly harnessed.
3. Sin degrades our brain potential through neuroplasticity, neurogenesis, and neural epigenesis.
4. Brain development technology is best used within the model provided in the Bible.

"Jesus grew ..."

From my twenty-first-century perspective, the adolescent Jesus was developing his brain as he listened and asked questions. The mystery of the Christian faith is that Jesus was fully human and fully God. Scripture tells us that Jesus was "the image of the invisible God, the firstborn over all creation" (Colossians 1:15) and that Jesus was "like his brothers in every way" (Hebrews 2:17), which would include his brain. As I respectfully apply modern knowledge of the brain to Jesus, my appreciation of him has grown. This perspective shines new light on his lessons and helps me better understand and deepen my relationship with him.

I believe one reason Jesus was fully human was so that he could be an example to us of how to live because how we live develops our brains. Asking, "What would Jesus do?" is crucial to our brain health and development. Considering

Jesus from this perspective can provide guidance about how each of us can support the development of our brains so that we may "have life, and have it to the full" (John 10:10).

Can We Really Study the Brain of Jesus?

Not directly, but we can study his words and behavior and the effect that Jesus had on others. Words and behavior reflect the development of the brain. Similarly, the ways Jesus affected others can give us clues as to how he can help us develop our brains.

There's no person in history whose words and behavior have been more carefully studied than Jesus. Pastors, priests, and theologians routinely infer beyond Jesus' words and behavior to better understand his meaning. I want us to go further and use Jesus' words, behavior, and his effects on others to help us understand his brain as an example of how our brains should develop.

I believe that following the example of Jesus can facilitate the healthy development of our brains. In my own life and in my approach to counseling, I use examples of Jesus' words and behavior to promote healthy brain development.

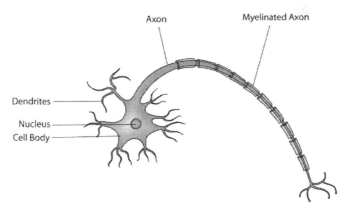

FIGURE 1. NEURON

Figure 1 is a drawing of a simple neuron in Jesus' brain. The cell body is grayish-pink, and if the axon is coated with myelin, it's white. This is the cell in the brain that conducts electrical impulses that produce thinking, feeling, vision, touch, movement, and so forth.

A thousand different types of neurons are found throughout the body, wherever communication needs to take place. Each neuron does this by signaling with an electrical impulse that begins in the cell body and travels down the axon, where the signal is passed by a very rapid chemical transfer across a tiny gap to the next neuron.

Of course, if we accept that Jesus was fully human and had a fully human brain, figure 1 is a drawing of a neuron in your brain, too. The basic components of Jesus' brain and your brain are identical.

The number of neurons in the human brain vary from approximately 85 billion to 200 billion, based on the age of the person. The brain starts to grow very rapidly twenty-one days after conception and into early childhood. We add new neurons rapidly in the first few years and slowly thereafter, but we also lose neurons that aren't being used. While we can't say precisely,[4] it appears that we lose approximately 40 percent of our brain's neurons from childhood to age sixty or seventy,[5] when we're left with about 85 to 90 billion neurons. [6, 7] Using the most reliable studies currently available, we can estimate that Jesus had 120 billion neurons in his brain when he was born. When he was crucified in his mid-thirties, his brain had approximately 100 billion neurons, each of which had an average of 10,000 connections with other neurons.

So My Brain Is Just Like Jesus' Brain?

No, your brain is different from Jesus' brain because Jesus cared for his brain as we cannot care for ours. The Bible tells us that only Jesus was perfectly faithful to his brain's design: "For we do not have a high priest who is unable to empathize with our weaknesses, but we have one who has been tempted in every way, just as we are—yet he did not sin" (Hebrews 4:15).

No matter how hard we try, none of us can attain perfection. We can eat the right foods, think the right thoughts, do the right deeds, and meditate on Scripture all day, but we'll still fall short of perfection.

Genesis, the first book of the Bible, tells us why this is so. The biblical narrative describes how the first humans chose not to obey God and exercised their own will. This separation from God produced important changes in their brains. Christianity, Islam, and Judaism use the word *sin* to describe violation of our relationship with God.

The idea of sin is an example of how neuroscience can inform faith. As we think of the brain, it's useful to think of sin as degrading our brain's potential. When we don't honor our relationship with God, several mechanisms degrade our brain and cause us to fall short of our potential. Our brain has grown differently than Jesus' brain because he was perfectly faithful to his brain's design and we have not been perfectly faithful.

Neuroscience has established that everything we say and do affects brain development.[2] The relationship is bidirectional; behavior affects brain development and brain development affects behavior. In fact, we now routinely use behavior to accurately infer underlying brain function[8] and brain pathology.[9] Brain pathology can be caused by a disease or a stroke or an injury such as a concussion, all of which disturb brain function and affect our observable behavior. Let me give you an example.

I have a good friend, Russ, who at age thirty-nine began to have signs and symptoms of early onset Parkinson's disease. Almost twenty years later, his use of medicine and a deep-brain stimulator help him to remain active and engaged (though his golf swing is worse than ever).

Every six months, Russ has his stimulator adjusted. At the clinic, his treatment team observes his behavior and administers a structured interview. Based on this information, they make inferences about his brain function and may adjust his brain stimulator and medications. They don't need to do a scan of Russ's brain because research on people with Parkinson's disease allows them to infer his brain-behavior links.[10-13] Russ's clinicians can make accurate inferences of his brain function because his observable behavior and reports from Russ and his wife reflect what is going on in his brain.[14]

We can infer what Russ's brain, my brain, your brain, and Jesus' brain are doing because all our behaviors are based on corresponding **neural networks**,[15-18] the organized links of neurons that develop based on experience. These networks are the basis of distinct brain patterns that can dominate our thinking and behavior.

> **Neural Networks**
> Organized links of neurons developed by experience.

We can think of our brains as pattern-making, pattern-seeking, and pattern-completing machines.[19] These patterns make us unique and are the basis of our feelings, thoughts, memories, attitudes, and habits.[18, 20, 21] Every choice you make changes your brain. Constantly changing with experience,[22] neurons develop networks with other nearby neurons and with distant brain regions and nervous system structures. [2] The neural networks and patterns can be extremely complex and may have a particular shape that depends on, for example, what we're viewing.[23] Repeated behaviors give rise to distinctive patterns of connections among brain regions.[24-27] Well-developed habits become difficult to change because they are represented in the brain by dominant neural networks.

The three most important mechanisms through which your brain develops neural networks are *neuroplasticity, neurogenesis,* and *neural epigenesis.*

Operating rapidly and very susceptible to outside influences, neuroplasticity is the constant pruning and linking of neurons. [28-31] Neural pruning and linking is occurring right now as you read this, helping you organize and store what you're learning so you can recall it later.

> **Neuroplasticity**
> Constant pruning and linking of neurons that mold the brain in response to experience.

Pruning and linking aren't haphazard; they're guided by experience. Neuroplasticity is called "experience-dependent plasticity"[2] because repeated experiences strengthen linkages among involved neurons and allow linkages with uninvolved neurons to die. Neurons that are well-linked to other neurons by repeated experiences are more resilient than neurons that don't have many linkages.[32] Neurons without many linkages tend to wither and die.[33]

Neurons will link up with other neurons whenever we repeat a thought or action. Neuroplasticity harnesses neurons together as we practice vocabulary words,[34] participate in pornography [35] and video games,[36] or practice the guitar.[37] The combination of linking and pruning strengthens the repeated word meanings, sexual or competitive fantasies, or fret fingering while weakening those that aren't practiced. Your brain is molded by what you practice, which is both bad and good. The bad news is that your brain is molded by your sin and forces outside of your control. The good news is that you can intentionally harness your neuroplasticity by focusing your attention and making proper choices. Your brain is always under development, a process that never stops and in which you can actively participate.

Neurogenesis has to do with neuron birth and development. Just twenty-one days after conception, your brain began to develop

> **Neurogenesis**
> The birth and growth of new neurons.

as a tube of neurons growing from stem cells. Millions of new neurons were created every hour and began migrating up your neural tube to organize your brain.

Just like Jesus, you had about 120 billion neurons when you were born. A few years ago, scientists thought we were born with all the neurons we would ever have and couldn't grow new neurons. We now know new neurons are always developing.[38] It takes about three weeks for a stem cell to develop into a mature neuron and begin to link up with other neurons. Neurogenesis in the adult brain occurs primarily in two brain structures, one of which is the hippocampus,[39] a major site of Alzheimer's disease,[40] and also occurs to a limited extent after a stroke or brain injury.[38]

Neuroscientists are exploring how stress and depression limit neurogenesis and may accelerate dementia.[41] Neurogenesis is vulnerable to chronic, sustained stress, which causes developing neurons to wither and die. It appears that the degrading effects of sin on neurogenesis can occur through the stress of living out of relationship with God. If we can protect neurogenesis, it can become an important road to recovery from depression[42] and may be helpful in treating other mental illnesses.

Epigenesis is the switching on or off of genetic code in cells, including neurons, based on life experiences.[2, 43-46] Research on neural epigenesis has revealed that early stressful experiences can cause enduring changes in brain health and function[47-49] that may be passed down to the next generation.[50-53] Genetic predispositions in neurons are expressed or lay dormant based on whether stressful experiences trigger epigenesis. Neural epigenesis is part of the reason that one identical twin develops a genetic psychological disorder such as schizophrenia or depression and the other twin does not.[48]

> **Epigenesis**
> Switching on or off of genetic code by life experiences.

During pregnancy and throughout life, stress-triggered epigenesis is implicated in differences in temperament and personality, susceptibility to depression and anxiety disorders,[54, 55] and the onset of many fatal diseases and dementias.[56] The warning from God in the Ten Commandments of punishment for "the sin of the parents to the third and fourth generation of those who hate me" (Exodus 20:5) is expressed by neural epigenesis. But just as sin can degrade the brain through neural epigenesis, loving caregivers can cause positive epigenetic changes, especially early in life. [45, 57-59] The promise in Exodus 20:6 of God "showing love to a thousand generations of those who love me and keep my commandments" harnesses neural epigenesis to repair poor parenting and provide a legacy to the next generation more valuable than material wealth.

Neuroplasticity, neurogenesis, and neural epigenesis can be used to improve brain function. What's especially exciting is that these brain mechanisms can be harnessed by counseling. The leading graduate school textbook of neuroscience reports, "It is intriguing to think that insofar as psychotherapy is successful in changing behavior it does so by producing alterations in gene expression."([56] page 1517)

What's most exciting to me is the idea that God designed our brains so we could *participate* in our neurorehabilitation. For example, we can choose to look at something and thereby change the involved neural networks and their neural patterns.[60-62] If we look at something often enough, a neural pattern develops that's dedicated to what we're seeing. The visual pattern triggers distinct emotional patterns, and the emotional patterns trigger distinct behavioral patterns. We usually think of these as habits. The brain's problem with pornography is not that the nude body is attractive to look at, it's how frequently we look so that it becomes a habit. My brain was designed so that I should be aroused by my wife in the context of God's created reality that requires I act so as not to become attracted to the beauty of other women. This is called spiritual discipline, for which we need a universal standard, inspired examples of which are found in the Bible, most notably in the life and teachings of Jesus.

We need to take care of our brains following guidelines proven to be brain-protective. The guidelines I try to follow are those Jesus followed. He protected and nourished his brain so it developed optimally even though he sometimes was severely stressed.

How Can Jesus Guide Me?

After accepting that the brain of Jesus had the same design as yours, can you accept the idea that Jesus' rejection of sin protected and developed his brain, allowing the brain-development processes to operate perfectly? Would you be willing to apply these to yourself now, intentionally developing your brain as Jesus developed his? We can learn a lot about how to develop our brains by paying attention to Jesus.

As a young psychologist exploring the claims of Jesus, I noticed that something amazing took place in the brains of his disciples in the brief time they were with him. Out of the twelve men Jesus recruited, eleven devoted their lives to him. Because they insisted Jesus was God, they were considered blasphemers by the religious authorities. The punishment for blasphemy was death, often by stoning or crucifixion. Putting aside the lapsed disciple Judas Iscariot, seven of the eleven remaining disciples died horrible deaths at the hands of the religious authorities because they kept insisting Jesus was God.

I asked myself, *How were their brains rehabilitated so quickly?* To rehabilitate someone presumes that the person's life has been degraded through illness, injury or habit and requires restoration. Jesus knew that their habits of cultural life reflected in their attitudes, values, and thinking were based in well-developed neural networks. Jesus changed his disciples' brains by offering a new life within the context of God's trustworthy love.

Jesus told them that trustworthy love begins with God: "Love the Lord your God with all your heart and with all your soul and with all your mind. This is the first and greatest commandment. And the second is like it: Love your neighbor as yourself" (Matthew 22:37–40). Jesus based loving ourselves and others on loving God, the trustworthy love that's the ideal for which our brain was designed; this is how our brain develops optimally.

It's not a coincidence that our brain prospers with trustworthy love[63-72] and develops poorly without trustworthy love.[73-78] Many studies of the brains of neglected or abused children demonstrate this. Numerous studies of rehabilitation from serious addiction[171-177] demonstrate that trustworthy love is the key ingredient. What's best for brain health and fitness is the trustworthy love that's central to God's character. Our brain naturally supports redemption and rehabilitation, with God's trustworthy love as the foundation, made personally available to each of us in a relationship with Jesus.

Jesus changed brains through relationships rather than by just preaching, which is a wonderful example for us all. We now know our brains are integrated with others' brains, influencing and being affected by the brains of those closest to us.[47, 79] By how we live, the examples we set for others influence how others live, and their brains change to reflect our participation in their lives. We will explore this important topic in the next chapter.

Why Should We Follow Jesus' Example?

Because our brain is always open to experience and the examples of significant others, we need to be intentional about how we guide its development. As you have learned, neuroplasticity, neurogenesis, and neural epigenesis can be hijacked by outside forces and we can get sloppy about how we allow our brains to be influenced. It's good that we now know this, but what are we going to do about it? Neuroscience is telling us how we *can* develop the brain, but we need first to understand how we *should* develop the brain. The example provided by Jesus and the guidance in the Bible are crucial.

The pace of neuroscience is rapidly accelerating and recently has begun to consider the effects of religious practices.[80] Ten years ago, the typical brain imaging study included only a few subjects, with only one imaging technology that was used to study only one area of the brain. Since then, we have undertaken huge studies of the "connectome,"[27, 49, 81, 82] in which many regions of the brain are studied simultaneously, with multiple technologies and hundreds of subjects. Several different connectome projects are underway, using different technical approaches. The 1000 Functional Connectomes Project[81] is studying 1,414 subjects using resting-state fMRI, functional magnetic resonance imaging. Using multiple brain imaging methods, the Human Connectome Project[25, 27] is studying 1,200 identical and fraternal twins and their siblings to search for patterns that may indicate brain dysfunction. What's most amazing is that the targeting of specific neurons in a living brain is now possible with *optogenetics*. Optogenetic technology[83] uses light to stimulate individual neurons and small groups of neurons. With this new technique, we can study their purpose with a degree of specificity not considered possible just a few years ago.

Every year, thousands of studies are rapidly adding to our knowledge of brain composition, structure, and function. The neuroscientific data acquired in the last five years already dwarfs all that we had previously collected. The information emerging from these studies will affect every area of human life. This research has spawned many different brain development technologies that are becoming widely available.[28, 84] They offer a reasonable alternative to medication in some cases and can be a helpful addition to psychotherapy.[85, 86] I advocate a careful approach to these technologies out of respect for their power. I am delighted that they are available, and I use some myself and recommend them to my clients, but I undertake brain development with caution.

I keep coming back to the lessons of Jesus and using Jesus' brain as a model for brain development because Jesus harnessed his brain's developmental capacity *in tune with God's perfect will for his life*. He achieved the potential of his perfect brain because he was faithful to his brain's design.

Your brain, the most efficient, powerful, delicate, resilient, and sophisticated organism on the planet, is your greatest responsibility. It's how you can become aware of God and your separation from God and how you can reconnect with God. It allows you to sense eternity. It's where your emotions, thoughts, and behaviors begin. It's where your relationships begin and end. It takes care of you better than you take care of it. It's what gets you into trouble and helps you to avoid trouble. Your brain is your constant companion.

If you're like me, you have taken your brain for granted for most of your life, until now. Well, get ready! You're in for an exciting experience as we explore your brain and how you can participate in its development, which is what I believe God intended.

Thank you for sticking with me as we moved through some occasionally difficult neuroscience. I hope the bibliographic references were helpful rather than distracting. I would like to provide you with the scientific underpinnings for the expansion of your appreciation of Jesus, perhaps echoing my experience. To set the stage for exploring how you can participate with God in developing your faithful brain, here are a few key takeaways.

Chapter Takeaways

1. Jesus' perfect human brain is a model for us to follow.
2. We can understand Jesus' brain by carefully studying his words and behavior and how he affected those closest to him.
3. The study of Jesus' brain can be a form of worship.
4. Neuroplasticity and neurogenesis are brain process we can harness and must protect.
5. Epigenesis is a natural biological process affected by our experiences, especially trauma.
6. Brain development technology is best used within the model provided in the Bible and with the example set by Jesus.

Discussion Questions

1. What are your thoughts about using Jesus' behavior and lessons to develop your brain?
2. Does looking at the life and lessons of Jesus from a neuroscience perspective impact how you think about your relationship with him? If so, how?
3. What were your character scores on the Faithful Brain Fitness Assessment in comparison to Jesus? What might you work on developing further?

CHAPTER 3

A Faithful Brain Is God-Integrated

> Love the Lord your God with all your heart and with all your soul and with your entire mind. This is the first and greatest commandment. And the second is like it: Love your neighbor as yourself.
>
> —*Matthew 22:37–39*

Brain Basics

1. Your brain is the center of your mind, integrated with your heart and soul.
2. A faithful brain is fully integrated with God, within itself, and with others.
3. A faithful brain optimizes its design, operating efficiently and maintaining resilience.
4. Your brain functions best when it's fully integrated with God and others in loving relationships.

Ripples of Sin

Carol is a smart, well-dressed, thirty-year-old, single registered nurse who comes to my office reporting problems with self-confidence, anxiety, and insomnia. These began three months before, stemming from an unwanted relationship at her hospital with a physician who was married. "We were friends and coworkers, but I definitely didn't want to be involved with a married man. I thought I made it real clear. But I made the mistake of accepting his help when I moved into my new apartment. He and several other coworkers helped me for a few hours one Saturday, and then basically, he just started pursuing me. He won't take no for an answer! I guess I shouldn't have encouraged him."

"How did you encourage him?"

"I accepted his help moving, and I should have known he'd expect more in return than I was willing to give. He leaves me sticky notes on the charts we're working on together. He touches me when and where I don't want to be touched. It's now to the point where when we're working on a patient, he moves so that he can look down my shirt or check out my bottom. It's disgusting, and I've told him to stop and back off a hundred times, but he just winks and smiles! I talked with the head nurse, who said she noticed that something was wrong but wondered what I had done to draw his attention, almost like I had seduced him! Now I'm starting to wonder if I did, but I dress like all the other nurses, and I've never even hinted that we could be anything other than coworkers.

"I don't know what to do. I feel confused and guilty and embarrassed. I need this job, but he's the head of the department, so he's always going to be there. If I keep bringing it up to my boss, it'll only make things worse."

Where is sin in this scenario? Does sin have to do with Carol seducing the physician? No, it seems likely that she hadn't. Carol is being buffeted by the ripples of sin from the physician. What's the best way to handle how another's bad behavior affects us? This chapter explains how faith in God helps us handle something like this.

What's the Bottom Line?

When Jesus was asked, "What's the bottom line? What's most important to understand?" he responded, "Love the Lord your God with all your heart and with all your soul and with your entire mind ... and love your neighbor as yourself."

Neuroscience supports the Bible's integrated and indivisible approach to the human person, including our brain.[47] We're designed to be completely and fully integrated beings[87, 88] with a soul into which we grow. Our brain's importance is apparent when we realize that its biology and physiology are the foundation of our emotions, thoughts, and behaviors.[2] Our brain develops and operates optimally when integrated with God, within itself, with our heart, throughout our body, and with other people.[79]

Vertical integration starts with God, extends into the cerebral cortex, down through the limbic system and brain stem and spinal cord, and into the vagal nervous system, integrating brain with heart and internal organs and synchronizing the autonomic nervous system. I believe this is where spiritual and emotional healing begins. Stephen Porges and his colleagues describe the "polyvagal" nervous system that supports our "social engagement system"[89, 90] by enervating our brain with the mouth, face, ears, heart, lungs, and genitals. Julian Thayer and his colleagues describe the "neurovisceral integration model"[91-94] that helps explain how the brain cooperates with the heart and viscera to maintain emotional balance. Their work has helped me to conclude that brain integration is best if it starts with God.

Horizontal integration has to do with the two hemispheres of the brain that are able to be dominant or submissive moment by moment and situation by situation. You function much better when they're integrated, as the perspective and emotion centered in the right brain is integrated with the language and logic of the left brain. Split-brain research was pioneered by Roger Sperry[95-99] and Michael Gazzaniga[100-105] at the California Institute of Technology. Their work on morality and the brain has contributed to my understanding of virtues, values, beliefs, and attitudes. Antonio and Hanna Damasio[106-111] at the University of Southern California have studied how emotions arise and help to define our conscious self. Their work has guided me as I consider how creativity, attitudes, beliefs, and morality can be affected by prayer.

Social integration has to do with how our brain is integrated with other brains. Daniel Siegel[112] and Louis Cozolino[113] firmly place our brain in our social context, described as "interpersonal neurobiology."[67, 114] Every human brain affects other brains with which it interacts.[115] Trusting relationships have pervasive protective effects on the brain[113] and allow us to become attuned to the brains of others.[116] Trust within teams, organizations, and among soldiers in battle stimulates brain activity in each participant. The interplay of love and trust with your neurobiology has been studied extensively by neuroscientists Sue Carter[66, 71, 117, 118] and Thomas Baumgartner.[119-121] Their work has helped me appreciate the brain-protective effects of loving relationships and points me back to Jesus' bottom line as expressed in Matthew 22 at the start of this chapter.

We will draw on the work of these researchers and many others as we learn that our brain functions best when it's fully integrated with our Creator, in our body, and with other people, in that order. As your brain becomes integrated, you move into synchrony with God's created reality. In synchrony with God's plan for your life, you become emotionally and physically healthier and more resilient.

We will also learn that when our brain is not fully integrated, it's out of synchrony with God's created reality, causing emotional and physical distress, illness, and premature death.

You are optimally resilient, creative, trustworthy, and loving when your brain is fully integrated because God designed you that way. When, like Carol, you're the victim of another person's sinful behavior, your faithful brain will help you avoid much of the misery that such a person can cause.

What's a Faithful Brain?

A faithful brain is one fully integrated with God, within itself, and with others, optimizing its design. It's the brain of a person who accurately reflects the image of God and accepts God's will for his or her life. It's a brain we may seek but will never perfectly develop. According to the biblical narrative, Jesus was the only person with a perfectly faithful brain. The brain of Jesus supported the ultimate human experience.

> **Faithful Brain**
> A brain that is fully integrated with God, within itself, and with others, optimizing its design.

Completely filled by God's purpose, Jesus can teach us how to develop a more faithful brain so we can "have life, and have it to the full" (John 10:10). Jesus guides us toward the optimal fit between each of our brains and God's creation. "If you hold to my teaching, you are really my disciples. Then you will know the truth, and the truth will set you free" (John 8:31–32). As we hold to his teachings, the truth that will set us free puts us in synchrony with God's design for creation and how we fit into his plans.

Living in synchrony with God's created reality allows us to develop our brain optimally because this is the context for which we were created. As we develop a more faithful brain under the influence of Jesus, his way of life helps us maintain optimal brain health and fitness.

How Does a Faithful Brain Develop?

In our relationships with Jesus, we do our best to adopt his values. We ask ourselves, "What would Jesus do?" and allow those thoughts to guide our choices. As we follow Jesus and live his way, neuroplasticity, neurogenesis, and neural epigenesis create predominant neural networks in our brain that are true to Jesus' character. The gradual development of our more faithful brain shows up in our developing character. As our character develops, we become more like Jesus.

The character of Jesus has many facets; we can call them character traits. Research has demonstrated that humans have twenty-four character traits.[122] These are organized in terms

Brain Integration	Character Trait
Vertical	Faith
	Hope
	Appreciation
	Gratitude
	Humor
	Humility
	Mercy
	Self-Control
	Prudence
	Vitality
	Dependability
	Bravery
	Persistence
Horizontal	Curiosity
	Open-Mindedness
	Love of Learning
	Perspective
	Creativity
Social	Love
	Kindness
	Social Intelligence
	Citizenship
	Fairness
	Leadership

of the hierarchy of faithful brain integration I use with my clients.[3]

We begin our vertical brain integration with God, developing faith, hope, appreciation, and gratitude for the gift of life and the sacrifice of his Son. The safety of our relationship with God helps us develop a lightness of being that we will call humor as the security of our place in God's created reality is revealed. Humility develops as we accept our place in God's plan, along with mercy as we realize we are all God's children. Self-control and prudence are the twin results of our awareness that we are stewards of God's planet and of humanity. Vitality and dependability are personal resources we cultivate to meet our responsibilities. Because God grants us the freedom to choose that also allows bad choices in ourselves and others, we develop bravery and persistence to meet these challenges.

The sufficiency of our horizontal brain integration depends on how well we develop our vertical integration. Horizontal brain character traits are more dependable if we first accept our place in God's created reality. We see this most clearly as we recognize unnecessary and unnatural boundaries to curiosity that come from traditions and other human endeavors. As we cultivate open-mindedness and love of learning, our perspective encompasses all of God's created reality, making our opportunities for creativity limitless.

Our social brain integration is based on our relationships with each other, as love, kindness, and social intelligence become hallmarks of our character. On this basis, we can safely and dependably practice citizenship and fairness as we

---

[3] We recently completed a study of 976 adults that found several of these traits correlated significantly with quality-of-life, described at www.faithfulbrain.com.

demonstrate faithful brain leadership, reflecting the image of God as we become fully integrated beings.

How Do I Interfere with Faithful Brain Integration?

According to the biblical narrative, as we separate from God and try to ignore or defy his created reality, we sin. From a brain-based perspective, sin interferes with heart, soul, and mind integration. In Curt Thompson's wonderful book *Anatomy of the Soul*,[123] he explained, "One way to comprehend the dynamic of sin is to see it as a matter of choosing to be mindless rather than mindful, which ultimately leads to our minds becoming disintegrated."

I want to use the hyphenated form of dis-integrated for emphasis. Sin leads to dis-integration of our brain from God. When we sin and give up brain integration with God, we lose synchrony with his created reality. Our brain becomes confused, less efficient, and more labored. We begin to lose our mind when we move away from God. One way to look at the physician who was harassing Carol is that he had lost his mind and jeopardized his family, career, and even his freedom. That makes sense when we think of his brain as becoming dis-integrated, in this case, dominated probably by his sexual desire. Healthy brain integration had been lost.

Brain dis-integration underlies most of our emotional troubles and interpersonal strife. It's what brings people to my office, reporting confusion and emotional pain. "I think I still love him, but I just can't get over how much he hurt me." "My wife complains that I compartmentalize my feelings and doesn't know whether she can trust me." "At first, it seemed like such a good idea, but the way things turned out, I should have tried to stop them."

These are recent statements from clients who profess faith in God but have had difficulty relying on God for direction. As we explored their stories, I found that their confusion was an early warning indicator of brain dis-integration, signaling separation from God. It may have been willful, but it was often accidental. It doesn't really matter; separation from God diminishes our brain in every way.

We separate from God and lose brain integration if we will not forgive and continue to resent, if we hurt others without recognizing their pain, if we gossip without care for the victim, and if we dodge responsibility for our addictions. I have been both perpetrator and victim of each of these sins.

Having struggled with sin over many years, I have learned that most of my confusion and emotional pain stemmed from going forward into the day without God, living life my way. Fortunately, because our brain was designed by God, we have the ongoing opportunity to reintegrate with his created reality. The grace Jesus reminds us is always available from our loving God is sufficient to reclaim the restorative capacities of our brain.

A helpful way to consider Carol's situation is that her confusion was an indication that she was losing her brain integration under assault from the physician. Carol's brain integration must start with God, but rather than drawing in close to God, Carol reported, "Well, I believe in God, but how's that going to help me here? I've got to figure out some way to handle this! I feel like I'm losing my mind!"

When I seek counseling for myself and when I offer counseling to clients such as Carol, the practice of faithful brain integration helps us deal with the consequences of sin—our own and others'. We begin faithful brain integration in the vertical plane by turning to God.

Carol had become separated from God, leading to confusion that can cause regret and guilt and embarrassment that can even lead to shame and self-disgust in a self-perpetuating cycle, as depicted in figure 2.

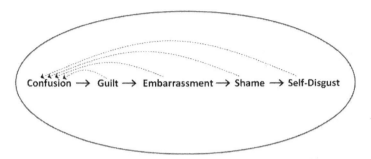

FIGURE 2. CORRECTIVE EMOTIONS CYCLE

Figure 2 depicts the increasing cycle of corrective emotions if they aren't addressed, which is often the case because they are painful. Corrective emotions such as guilt and regret can lead to emotional dis-integration and will become more painful and corrosive if we don't deal with them. Trying to ignore these emotions usually causes greater confusion, leading to escalation of pain, creating even more confusion.

Guilt and embarrassment focus on specific behaviors and choices, whereas shame focuses on the self. "I did something bad" is a guilty statement, and "I am a bad person" describes shame. Guilt is more likely to prompt an apology and attempt to make amends, whereas shame often leads to denial and self-justification.

The corrosive nature of shame has been identified in research.[124] Comparing guilt and shame, these researchers reported, "Moderately painful feelings of guilt about specific behaviors motivate people to behave in a moral, caring, socially responsible manner. In contrast, intensely painful feelings of shame don't appear to steer people in a constructive moral direction ... Rather than motivating reparative action, shame often motivates denial, defensiveness, anger, and aggression."

Shame is corrosive because of its effect on the brain, discoloring our personal story and wearing us down. It does this through the hippocampus, where information is temporarily stored before a small proportion is made into memories.[56] In addition to new information, an already-established memory is refreshed every time it's recalled; the hippocampus refreshes the neural network devoted to that memory.[125] Our memories are never permanent[126] because they constantly are being refreshed, which originates in our hippocampus.[127] If we recall a shameful memory without the proper perspective, we can cause it to be refreshed with more shame than it originally contained. This is the basic problem with many emotional disorders, including anxiety, reactive depression, and post-traumatic stress disorder.

I use the term *hippocampal rehearsal* (HR) to explain this to my clients. HR is an automatic process constantly recreating our personal story, revising and reinforcing memories. When we think shameful thoughts, hippocampal rehearsal taints our story, storing the memory with the stain of shame. In this way, shame gradually wears us down, shrinks our hippocampus,[128] and sets us up for chronic depression and other serious mental illnesses.[129] HR gradually causes us to believe that we're less competent, inadequate, less lovable, and worthwhile.

God's love is the most powerful antidote to self-destructive hippocampal rehearsal. The apostle John said,

> God is love. Whoever lives in love lives in God, and
> God in them. This is how love is made complete

among us so that we will have confidence on the day of judgment: In this world we are like Jesus. There is no fear in love. Perfect love drives out fear, because fear has to do with punishment. (1 John 4:17–18)

We must start faithful brain development by turning to God because this is where we find spiritual salvation, emotional restoration, and brain health and fitness.[130] Becoming infected by God's love, we find it easier to participate in our own emotional rehabilitation.

How Did You Help Carol?

I helped Carol begin to restore her faithful brain by reorienting to her brain's Designer. We started with a prayer that God would guide her back to emotional health and provide clarity about what to do. Prayer is helpful when we have a secure relationship with God, but it's problematic when we have an insecure or avoidant relationship.[131]

As a Christian psychologist, I was able to explore this with Carol and helped her clarify her relationship with God. She explained that she considered God as real but had difficulty with the father image due to problems as a girl with her biological father. She had been held to strict standards of behavior enforced with corporal punishment that she thought was unfairly apportioned among her siblings. She recognized that this was contaminating her spiritual development and asked me to help her reestablish a trusting love relationship with God. We prayed together and I also encouraged her to discuss this with her pastor. From my perspective, emotional and mental health can be greatly facilitated by participation in a healthy church community.

I encouraged Carol to continue to actively reintegrate with God through prayer and Bible study. In addition, I assigned her to read *What's So Amazing About Grace?* by Philip Yancey,[132] and we discussed one chapter each week, integrating it into her therapy.

I used the simple model in figure 2 to help Carol understand that confusion builds as we try to avoid the corrective emotions. We explored Carol's confusion and feelings of regret and guilt. We discussed how her appraisal of the situation was creating guilt.

As clarity replaced confusion, Carol carefully considered her guilt. "I honestly don't know if I did anything to cause this, but even if I did, I've been very clear about not wanting him to continue. Very clear!" Since guilt indicated "I've done something wrong," she began to understand that any embarrassment she might continue to feel was unnecessary and was a consequence of a situation that she was trying to remedy. Although she resented that she was caught in a situation created by another's sin, she became resolute and more confident.

Most important, Carol avoided falling into self-destructive shame that indicated "I'm a bad person." If we get stuck in shame, its paralyzing nature requires God's healing grace to release us so we can resolve our confusion and take appropriate action. Within the context of God's grace, we can more clearly see guilt when we're responsible and begin to take action. Apologizing, making amends, and restoring trust are more likely when we surrender and accept God's grace and guidance.

As Carol began to get reoriented to God's direction for her life, I helped remedy her insomnia, anxiety, unhealthy hippocampal rehearsal, and eroding self-confidence by using four components of a faith-based approach to cognitive behavioral therapy called brain-based Christian counseling (BBCC).[4] The interventions I used with Carol are descried below.

Brain Restorative Sleep

Due to the stress of her situation, Carol had not been sleeping well. The adult brain needs five cycles of about ninety minutes each of deep, restful sleep for housekeeping and to maintain its health. For adults, that's seven to eight hours, but the necessary sleep duration is a function of sleep quality. Restless or anxious sleep is not brain restorative. If you've had enough high-quality sleep, you will awaken spontaneously with your thoughts consolidated and clarity developing, ready for a successful day. It had been several months since she had experienced deep and restful sleep and had awakened feeling refreshed and clear.

Brain-restorative sleep is a "keystone habit"[133] that leads to the development of other habits that are brain protective and brain restorative. I helped Carol develop her brain-restorative sleep habit using guidelines that you can find on our website. Some of the most important for Carol were the timing of caffeine and sugar intake, regular sleep-assisting exercise, and prayers of gratitude.[134-136] I also helped her develop her personal prayer relaxation skills.

Personal Prayer Relaxation

Carol was tense, anxious, and irritable. The degree of relaxation available to each of us depends on how well our

---

[4] Free resources describing these interventions are available at www.faithfulbrain.com.

brain is integrated with God and with our body. To facilitate this, I helped Carol develop a practice of prayer that would include a word or phrase that recalled an episode in her life when she was safe, comfortable, relaxed, and aware of God's presence in her life. She chose "Grandpa's swing"; recalling summer vacations as a girl visiting her grandparents' farm. I helped her link this phrase and memories of the episode to exhalation of her breath during a progressive muscle-relaxation exercise.[91, 137-140] We then expanded the recollection to make it multi-sensory, including the rustle of leaves and the warm breeze of the day, the smell of new-cut grass, and hearing goats, sheep, and chickens in the background. As she prepared to drop off to sleep, I asked her to offer a prayer of thanksgiving and gratitude followed by "Grandpa's swing" to facilitate her transition to deep, restful sleep.

Prayers of gratitude can be very healthy.[135, 136, 141] An advantage of using a trigger word or phrase during such a bedtime prayer is that it can be used at other times to connect with God and diminish autonomic nervous system arousal. Whether preparing for sleep, awakening during the night, or encountering her victimizer during the day, Carol used "Grandpa's swing" to remind her of God's presence, trigger her relaxation to help with anxiety, and thereby calm her anxious reaction. This also helped her insomnia as a component of brain-restorative sleep.

Goaling

We all need a purpose in life that's greater than ourselves. One way to develop this is through the Goaling process. I began this near the end of our first session by asking, "What do you want most out of life?" Carol was surprised that I wanted to ask her about something other than her symptoms and her problems with self-confidence, anxiety, and insomnia. I explained I wanted to not only help her *feel better* but also to help her *get better*, and we would be pursuing both.

Goaling helps a person become engaged in a valued future. If you recall Peter's story from chapter 1, when we turn toward the future, we turn away from our past, harnessing the brain's built-in capacities to stick with healthy choices. Over the next three sessions, Carol developed her prioritized Goaling Life Plan. I helped her identify a list of twenty people with whom to share her life plan. At first, she couldn't imagine trusting twenty people to know her at that level of transparency, but she gradually gained confidence and began to appreciate the importance of both accountability partners and fulfillment partners in overcoming inertia and turning her life toward a greater purpose.

Happy Hippocampus Exercise

To help Carol boost her self-confidence, I administered the Character Strengths Rating Scale and taught her the Happy Hippocampus Exercise. This is aimed directly at reversing her self-destructive hippocampal rehearsal. On the rating scale, she compared her character with Jesus across twenty-four character traits and selected *bravery* to work on: "Confronting threats, challenges, difficulties, fear, or pain; speaking up for what is right when there is opposition; acting on unpopular convictions. Not the absence of fear."

I asked Carol to make this commitment: "As you prepare for bed each night, find three episodes during the day in which you were more brave than you were yesterday. Before you drop off to sleep, briefly bring them to mind and thank God for those opportunities."

Her homework was to do that every night for the next week, until we met again. At the next session, we reviewed her progress. She told me, "Some days, it got to be late in the day and I hadn't done anything that was brave, so I had to come up with something. Usually it wasn't much but I was amazed that I could, even helping some of my friends be more brave!" The Happy Hippocampus Exercise is a positive psychology intervention[142, 143] that depends on

1. Intentionally providing focused information to your hippocampus before you drop off to sleep. The hippocampus is the doorway to your autobiographical brain, transferring less than 1 percent of the information it processes into long-term memories that describe you to yourself. By placing the examples of bravery in her hippocampus at a time when the information doesn't have much competition, Carol was more likely to harness her neuroplasticity to develop the neural networks that contain the memories of her bravery, gradually changing her self-narrative.
2. Helping us recognize we may have more of a character trait than we might otherwise believe. This was certainly the case with Carol. "I just didn't realize that I had a lot more courage than I was giving myself credit for. Once I started paying attention, it was right there! The only hard part was trying to be braver today than I was yesterday." The change in her narrative must be recognized by Carol so that self-efficacy can be established.[144, 145]
3. Encouraging us to step beyond our usual comfort zone to try something new, with each new behavior harnessing neuroplasticity in the service of developing a character trait. As Carol got to the end of the day

and hadn't had the opportunity to be "more brave today than yesterday," she began to create such opportunities. Following through on her homework was an important part of her therapy. Homework is an often overlooked but key part of cognitive behavior therapy.[146] Behavior-change homework that improves positive emotional affect and optimism helps people build the healthy habits that create resilience.[143]

Carol's perception of her bravery changed radically within a few weeks, in part because she began to recognize that bravery was already part of her character. She also enjoyed taking a closer look at her relationship with Jesus. "Thinking about how some of his character had rubbed off on me was pretty neat. I really saw how Jesus has been influencing me more than I had imagined."

Taking these steps, Carol was quickly able to improve her anxiety and insomnia. Her self-confidence developed slowly but surely. She began to realize she needn't feel guilty or embarrassed about this situation; she had been caught in the ripples of another's sin.

Carol began to explore formal legal action against the physician and her employer, but she was ambivalent. "His wife is a wonderful person, and he's got grown kids who'd be horrified if they knew how their father acted. I just don't want to hurt them." I suggested that she talk in confidence with her pastor and develop a biblical perspective that was broader than what I was competent to offer.

After consultation with her pastor, Carol decided to take formal action against the physician, but she couldn't find any coworkers who would join her. However, two former nurses at the hospital and a physician's assistant were willing to confirm her reports of the offending physician's behavior and the difficult work environment this created.

Carol retained an attorney who counseled her about what she could expect if she moved forward. Her excellent work history allowed her to choose to leave the hospital and work for a home-health agency across town. In her hospital exit interview, she described once again to her supervisor the physician's pattern of behavior and asked that it be investigated.

After not hearing anything from her former employer for three months, Carol's attorney wrote a letter to the physician and hospital administrator that immediately brought action. She stopped short of filing a lawsuit after receiving a personal letter of apology from the physician and her nurse supervisor, and a promise from the hospital administrator that the physician would be reprimanded and required to participate in counseling.

Though she hadn't asked for it, Carol was offered an opportunity to return to her former position with a salary increase, but she declined.

Why Must I Start with God?

Integration begins with God so we can be realigned with God's created reality. This is another way to consider Jesus' instructions that we are to love God with all our heart and soul and with our entire mind. Sin separates us from God, disrupts brain integration, and makes it easier to separate from God even further. As we sin, we spiral away from the purpose for which we were designed, fitting in to God's created reality. Although we will never achieve a perfectly faithful brain, inviting God to help us develop and maintain brain integration is a necessary and effective first step.

As we look at how Carol was helped to deal with her situation, it's important to recognize that we started with her vertical integration, taking a top-down approach. She began by reconnecting with and becoming reoriented to God. This first step is crucial and sometimes bypassed as people move to horizontal integration and try to depend on their own resources to devise a new solution or move to social integration in which they seek the support of others to come up with a solution. These must come after we have reconnected with God.

In emergencies, and when we're feeling threatened, we tend to miss the efficacy of God and rely on our resources and on those close to us or on people we recognize as experts. We have a sense of desperate urgency that drives us to take action and miss the most powerful action we could take—asking God to step into our emergency. Taking this step first allows God to guide all the integration that follows. Taking this step first also helps with clarity and gives us security, both of which are important for survival and resilience. I have been involved with thousands of people in desperate situations, facing horrible losses and fearsome threats, but I have never been disappointed when we began our vertical integration with God.

Chapter Takeaways

1. Your brain is the center of your mind, integrated with your heart and soul.
2. A faithful brain is fully integrated with God, within itself, and with others.

3. A faithful brain optimizes its design, operating efficiently and maintaining resilience.
4. A faithful brain is degraded by sin, which saps its energy and potential.
5. Separation from God opens us to brain dis-integration.
6. Brain dis-integration is signaled by confusion that can cycle out of control.
7. A faithful brain helps us fit into God's created reality.

Discussion Questions

1. How was Carol's brain's integration with God impacted by the doctor?
2. What are some things you can do to reintegrate your brain with God?
3. How often do you notice yourself doing negative hippocampal rehearsal?
4. How can you focus hippocampal rehearsal to positively harness your neuroplasticity?

CHAPTER 4

A Faithful Brain Is Relational

In the beginning was the Word, and the Word was with God, and the Word was God.
—*John 1:1*

Brain Basics

1. Thoughts and emotions are intertwined in the brain.
2. Memories are created by thoughts that have emotional salience or emphasis.
3. Without paying attention to its emotional salience, a message cannot be fully comprehended.
4. Your brain's ability to understand biblical lessons is enhanced by your relationship with Jesus.

Your brain was designed for relationships, beginning with a confident relationship with God, also known as faith. Your relationship with God is the template for your relationships with others. Healthy relationships provide the optimum context for brain health and the development of resilience. Integrated with God and others, your brain is designed to take care of you in a broken world.

"I Can't Stop Thinking about It!"

Charlie is a forty-one-year-old detective in a large metropolitan police department who is married to Sherry, a forty-year-old physical therapist. Charlie and Sherry are sitting comfortably together on my couch, with Sherry reporting that Charlie recently has become withdrawn, irritable, and easily angered.

"I have no idea what's bothering him. I really love him, and I want to get back to what we had! All he'll say is that it's about work. We've always talked things out before, but now he's just clammed up." They have three teenage daughters. "He'll barely talk to me, and he's almost completely stopped talking to the girls. It seems like he's avoiding them. He's never been that way with them."

"Charlie, do you notice the change in you that concerns Sherry?"

"Sure I do, and she's right," he says with irritation in his voice. "It's about work, and I can't talk about it!" Charlie's tone of voice tells me to stay away. He's polite, but his flaring nostrils communicate anger and something more that I will soon discover.

"Charlie, I know your work is confidential, so we'll leave that alone, but can you come in and talk with me privately about what's going on at home?"

"Sure, as long as we don't talk about work. Can't do that." Charlie has been a police officer for eighteen years and is proud of his work.

Over the next five weeks, Charlie cancels three appointments, always apologizing and giving work as the reason. In the interim, I learn from Sherry that Charlie is heading one of the teams working on a case that involves a serial rapist and killer that's all over the news. The manhunt has recently been concluded after an all-points bulletin resulted in the likely perpetrator being rescued from an angry mob by the police. He has been arraigned and is awaiting trial.

When I finally get to meet with Charlie, he looks tired and defeated. He tells me, "I'm not sleeping much or well. I use sleeping pills so I fall asleep, but I have a nightmare or wake up sweating and worried. I can't stop thinking about work. I even think about work when I'm surfing, and that's not like me!" Charlie has been a surfer all of his life and used to surf several days a week "to get out of my head." He hasn't been surfing for several months. "I just can't relax. I'm always tense, and I'm explosive. I can't believe how I'm treating the girls; I blow up over little things they do, normal girl stuff I used to think was cute, but now, almost everything they do makes me blow up!"

Post-traumatic stress disorder (PTSD) is a serious psychological problem that can happen to anyone, even battle-hardened soldiers and Marines, firefighters, and police officers. I'm pretty sure I know this is what's going on with Charlie, so I ask about the nightmares and intrusive thoughts.

"Okay, I can talk about it now because we got the bad guy, but I've never had something like this hit me so hard! I've dealt with a lot of terrible stuff, but this one really got to me. I had to interview a young woman and her husband this guy raped and shot. They both survived, but they're really messed up. She's just a few years older than my eldest, and she even looks like her! Every time I look at my girls, I think about her. He broke into their house in a nice neighborhood, and I can see her tied up and watching this guy shoot her husband and then everything else that happens! This is @#*%#!! I can't stop thinking about it! In the nightmares, it's like I'm stuck in cement and can't stop my family from being hurt! I really don't care about myself, but I can't stand the idea of them getting hurt! I wake up so pissed off that I just can't go back to sleep!"

"Do you think that's why you're avoiding your daughters?"

"Yeah, I suppose so, but then I also don't want to let them out my sight! I think about how this guy was raised. His favorite uncle used to brag to him about how he had abused women when he was a soldier. An American soldier! The guy's uncle was supposedly a Green Beret, and he's bragging about raping and killing women to his ten-year-old nephew! This world is so @#*%#!! Sometimes, I wish I'd never had kids! There's so many bad people! I don't trust anyone anymore! My wife and my partner and that's it!"

Charlie's brain has been hijacked by trauma. He meets the diagnostic criteria for post-traumatic stress disorder.[147] Although many people recover from PTSD without treatment,[148] it has seriously affected Charlie long enough that he needs to get himself into counseling.[149] Counseling is especially important when PTSD is caused by intentional trauma,[150] because hurting each other violates how our brain was designed. He also needs to improve his resilience so he can handle future trauma and work in law enforcement as long as wants rather than being forced to retire early.

We know more about how to treat PTSD than about how to improve psychological resilience so people don't develop it in the first place.[151, 152] The Comprehensive Soldier Fitness (CSF) program was implemented by the United States Department of Defense in 2009 to improve the resilience of American service members sent to combat in Iraq and Afghanistan.[153]

While CSF training has generally been well received and appears to be beneficial in many areas,[154] it has not been shown to be successful in the prevention of PTSD.[151] From my perspective, a key part of the problem is that integrating the soldier's faith as a resilience resource was watered down in CSF so that "spirituality" doesn't focus on God. As the CSF program defines this, "An individual's spirituality draws upon personal, philosophical, psychological, and/or religious teachings or beliefs, and forms the basis of their character." At the least, this is confusing because most Americans link their spirituality with God. At the worst, CSF training without a focus on God may supplant the faith that has been part of the warrior's resources throughout history.

The CSF approach to spirituality reflects how traditional American health care and the fields of psychology and psychiatry have kept faith partitioned from therapy.[140] I was trained and mentored to keep faith out of the counseling office, but my experience working with people like Charlie and thousands of others has turned me toward the integration of neuroscience and faith. As I have learned from soldiers returning from combat, a good chaplain can be very helpful in developing resilience and preventing trauma from hijacking a vulnerable brain.

By helping people develop faithful brains, victims of violent crime, accidents, and natural disasters and combat veterans who have PTSD can improve their resilience for future trauma. Our brains are designed for relationships; using our relationship with God as a template for healthy relationships with others develops resilient brains.

Properly trained Christian counselors and psychologists must take the initiative to counteract the partitioning of faith and neuroscience. In 2013, a few months after a monster tornado destroyed their elementary school in Moore, Oklahoma, I joined six of my former counseling students from Covenant Theological Seminary to work with forty teachers and staff from Plaza Towers Elementary School to psychologically prepare for the next school year. Our intent was to help them develop resilience focused on the importance of healthy relationships with each other and God. We were invited to do this through the initiative of one of my students whose personal experience recovering from trauma centered on developing her own relationship with God. Our intervention was a blend of faith and neuroscience, emphasizing the strong relationships each of them had for the others and how every one of us can have a safe, loving relationship with God.

We currently are working with Reboot Combat Recovery, a faith-based program supporting service members and families at the U.S. Army's Fort Campbell. This voluntary program takes a faith-based approach to developing resilience and post-traumatic growth. This initiative springs from the hearts of a young couple whose confident relationship with God led them to develop a popular and apparently effective alternative to traditional psychiatric and psychological treatment.

These programs integrate faith and neuroscience in settings that some believe should be off limits to faith practices. While I agree that public schools and army bases should not mandate one faith over another, this is where we find many people of faith who have been traumatized. Fort Campbell and the public school in Moore allowed their facilities to be used but provided no funding.

Evidence-based interventions combined with biblical lessons resonate with people of faith who are struggling with trauma. Faithful brain development can help people develop resilience, guided by the wisdom of the Bible.

How Does John 1:1 Guide Faithful Brain Development?

"In the beginning was the Word, and the Word was with God, and the Word was God" introduced Jesus as God available in human form to reveal the mind of God. Jesus' brain was the instrument to reveal the mind of God, with each of our brains capable of receiving his message optimally delivered in the context of our relationship with Jesus.

The full impact of God requires integration of your brain with Jesus' brain. This begins with language but goes far beyond, into experiencing Jesus with all your magnificent brain's capacity. Because Jesus is perfectly synchronized with God's created reality, you have an opportunity to align yourself with God's perfect will for your life through a relationship with Jesus.

Language is the brain's most important organizing strategy. Language, our use of words, helps us understand ourselves as we write our own stories. Language helps us understand others and is the most ready currency of our relationships. The developmental history of humanity has depended on language as the primary method of knowledge acquisition and transmission. Even within science and technology, mathematics and computer code are described as languages.

Language is not only our primary means for organizing our brains to appreciate and understand reality, it's also our primary means of *experiencing* reality.

One of the most important characteristics of your brain is how it intertwines language, thoughts, and emotions.[20, 107, 108, 155-158] We used to believe these were separate processes, but they're closely intertwined. While it's obvious that our thoughts and memories can trigger emotions, as far as neuroscientists can tell, every thought that becomes a memory has emotion tied to it. This is because the information tagged by your emotional circuits is more likely to be made into memories.

The tagging of thoughts with emotions is what psychologists call **emotional salience**,[159-162] the feelings attached to a thought. Without emotional salience, the information flowing into your brain forms a jumbled cloud. The emotional salience of a thought determines its importance and likelihood of recall. A thought with high emotional salience will be easily stored and recalled, but a thought without salience will be lost in the cognitive cloud and not formed into a useful memory.

The smell of oven-fresh baking powder biscuits triggers a smile and sixty-year-old memories of Sunday dinner at my grandmother's house

> **Emotional Salience**
>
> The power and resilience of a thought is supplied by its emotional tags.

because the original experience had strong emotional salience that was tagged to my memories of that day. Today, I actually re-experienced those Sunday dinners of long ago, triggered by my wife's efforts. When I bit into a baking powder biscuit with butter and orange marmalade, I re-experienced, not just recalled, the memory of my family around the dinner table. The emotional horsepower of that memory was strong enough to retrieve images, emotions, sounds, tastes, and smells. I was flooded with the experience—where I was sitting, the jokes and banter of people long gone, the smells and tastes of the foods, and my anticipation of Mom's homemade cherry pie topped with vanilla ice cream.

Negative emotions are also tied to thoughts and can trigger re-experiencing, which is why you shudder and your face grimaces when you recall an embarrassing memory.

In PTSD, painful memories of extreme violence intrude into your awareness and recreate a strong physiologic response triggered by otherwise neutral cues.

Because our brains are designed so that words can have emotional salience, emotions can be powerfully communicated by language. Words can be given deep meaning in many ways. [163-165] When spoken aloud, the intonation and stress of the words causes their meaning to deepen. The emotion we intend to attach to our words spoken to another can trigger emotions in them immediately and later when our words are recalled. When written, the poetic arrangement of words and their layout on the page can deepen their meaning.[166]

> i carry your heart with me (i carry it in
> my heart) i am never without it(anywhere
> i go you go, my dear; and whatever is done
> by only me is your doing, my darling)
>   i fear
> no fate (for you are my fate, my sweet) i want
> no world(for beautiful you are my world, my true)
> and it's you are whatever a moon has always meant
> and whatever a sun will always sing is you
>
> here is the deepest secret nobody knows
> (here is the root of the root and the bud of the bud
> and the sky of the sky of a tree called life; which grows
> higher than soul can hope or mind can hide)
> and this is the wonder that's keeping the stars apart
>
> i carry your heart (i carry it in my heart)

When words are combined with other sensory experiences, their meaning is expanded, such as the rhythm and melody of words in a musical score. The poetry of e. e. cummings spoken by a lover to his beloved and included with beautiful pictures and dramatic music carries even deeper meaning in this YouTube reference you may want to view.[167]

Words attached to movement, music, choreography, and drama are powerful. After only an hour of engagement with a skillfully crafted dramatic character, the actor's words and the words spoken to the actor create an emotional response in us because we are no longer merely viewing; we have become engaged emotionally and now participate in their drama.

How Does Emotional Salience Pertain to the Bible?

The relationship in your brain between words and emotions has implications for understanding the Bible. We will *experience* the Bible more fully if we integrate the strengths of the right and left hemispheres, as described in figure 3.

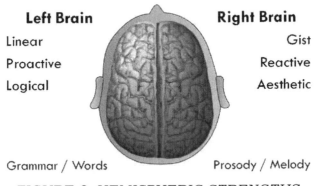

FIGURE 3. HEMISPHERIC STRENGTHS

If we explore the Bible using only our left-brain's linear and logical abilities, we can miss some of the emotional impact of the message. But if we experience the Bible using only our right brain's aesthetic abilities and its ability to quickly grab the gist of our experience, we can miss some of the deep meaning of the message and how it applies to our lives.

But if Bible study integrates our left brain with our right brain and our emotional limbic system, appreciation of the Bible's value in our daily lives is greatly enhanced. This is one of the reasons that worship songs are important in church services. Words engage primarily the left brain, while music engages primarily the right brain. We can experience the message more deeply when it's conveyed with words and music simultaneously, as this improves our horizontal integration. If we choose to sing, we are more likely to experience brain changes that improve the integration of the message into our lives.

In addition to songs and poetry, our relationships with others provide some of our most powerful emotional salience tags. Our brain links the content of a message with our emotional relationship with the messenger. A message delivered with love by someone we respect and trust will be interpreted by our brain differently from the same message delivered dismissively by someone we don't respect or trust. Because our thoughts are affected by our emotions, our experience of the message is affected by our relationship with the messenger. When emotional salience is attached to the messages of the Bible by our relationship with the messenger, our brains are better able to access its deep meaning. A good teaching pastor is a stand-in for Jesus, a fearsome responsibility!

When we consider the effect of relationships on how the brain processes information, "The Word became flesh," referring to Jesus, takes on additional meaning. A relationship with Jesus is an opportunity to fully understand the Bible. Our relationship with Jesus helps our relational brain become emotionally engaged with the biblical narrative, thereby enhancing and clarifying its meaning. Reading the Bible before I became a Christian and experiencing the Bible now supports this and is confirmed by others who have come to their faith in adulthood.

Jesus' spoken intonation and stress of the words deepened his disciples' understanding beyond what was recorded in the Bible. But far beyond Jesus' vocal presentation, the emotional salience of his messages was conveyed through his relationships with them.[5] Although his message seemed preposterous to many, the disciples accepted his words because they loved and trusted him. I can have this experience during Holy Communion if I am able to quiet my brain, settle into my relationship with Jesus, and recall his words. Before he was crucified, Jesus shared a last supper with his disciples and used the symbols of bread and wine to help give emotional salience to his upcoming sacrifice.

> And he took bread, gave thanks and broke it, and gave it to them, saying, "This is my body given for you; do this in remembrance of me." In the same way, after the supper he took the cup, saying, "This cup is the new covenant in my blood, which is poured out for you." (Luke 22:19–20)

In these moments, I am transported back more than 2,000 years to be present with him. Sometimes, I seem to hear his voice. Rather than just reading the words, I am experiencing the Bible.

---

[5] A sense of the power of the spoken Bible is available to modern listeners in *The Bible Experience* at www.BibleExperience.com.

How Can I Experience the Bible?

You can merely read the Bible, but a faithful brain integrated with God will help you to deeply experience the Bible. Within the context of a relationship with Jesus, your experience of the Bible will expand because your relational brain can help restore God's meaning to the written words.

Try this experiment. Read aloud three times "God is love" with a different vocal emphasis on each word. Christians usually experience increased positive emotional salience of the phrase over each recitation, broadening and deepening its meaning. This increase in positive emotional salience is a small example of how you can improve your experience of the Bible by paying attention to the emotional salience you have attached to the words.

Now, go back and repeat the exercise as if you were the evil one, Lucifer, or Demon Screwtape in C. S. Lewis's *Screwtape Letters*.[170] Read aloud three times "God is love" with a different vocal emphasis on each word, from the first through the third, but as if you detested the words. Notice the frustration building in you and how easily that's conveyed to the listener with your strained voice. This is because your brain was designed to fit into God's created reality, which is based on love as described in the Bible. You are straining to go against God's design of your brain.

The deep meaning of the Bible can be revealed through our relationships with others in our church community.[168, 169] As I listen to my friend Dale Tiemann read the words of the Bible at our worship services, I am transported by her love of God. She conveys to me her trust and love of the message because, through my relationship with her, I know of her relationship with God. My awareness of her relationships with God, Jesus, and the Holy Spirit helps me experience the message more deeply, which affects my understanding of the Bible.

Our emotional relationships with Jesus and with other Jesus followers can help fill the words of the Bible with their intended meaning. This is explained in the Gospels, when Jesus was asked by the disciples why he taught with parables, short stories that had layers of meaning. Jesus explained that a relationship with him was necessary to fully experience their meaning.

> This is why I speak to them in parables: Though seeing, they do not perceive; though hearing, they do not understand. In them is fulfilled the prophecy of Isaiah:
>
> *"You will be ever hearing but never understanding; you will be ever seeing but never perceiving. For these peoples' hearts have become calloused; they hardly hear with their ears, and they have closed their eyes. Otherwise they might see with their eyes, hear with their ears, understand with their heart and turn, and I would heal them."*
>
> But blessed are your eyes because they see, and your ears because they hear. For truly I tell you, many prophets and righteous people longed to see what you see but did not see it, and to hear what you hear but did not hear it. (Matthew 13:13–17)

The neuroscience of language processing helps us appreciate that Jesus' loving relationships with his disciples moved them closer to God's created reality and readied their brains to experience his parables' deeper meanings. The disciples were being shown by God in human form the necessary method to communicate meaning, one a relationship at a time. Jesus' humanity was necessary this lesson. The message and the messenger were completely integrated so that the meaning of the message was fully communicated.

If Jesus' words don't move you, please take another look at your relationship with him; they were never intended to be only read but fully experienced in the context of an active, personal relationship. This is the most important reason your brain was designed like Jesus' brain: his messages need to be received and interpreted by all the communication channels built in to your brain. Jesus helped his disciples tune into his brain. In this way, Jesus also has demonstrated to us how to tune into his brain. As Jesus followers, through our relationships we can extend God's love to others so we can all experience the Bible and the deep meaning of his lessons today.

How Did You Help Charlie?

At its most basic level, effective counseling depends on a healthy, trustworthy, and loving relationship. I am confident that when the Comprehensive Soldier Fitness program is analyzed by scientists, we will find that those components focused on improving healthy relationships are the most effective. This is the essence of Carl Rogers's client-centered therapy[171-173] and the powerful idea behind the success of Alcoholics Anonymous[174] and motivational interviewing, the most effective psychotherapy for alcohol dependence. [174-176] When each of us, especially someone who has been traumatized or shamed, feels love and acceptance from another person, something happens that goes beyond the best-researched techniques and treatments. It's as if both brains are engaged as God intended.

But, as William Miller, the developer of motivational interviewing, has written, "The strangely transforming power of love has been widely lauded for millennia, yet it is a concept often curiously absent in traditional psychology textbooks and clinical training."[177] The efficacy of the therapeutic relationship is acknowledged by every helping profession, but each profession studies, teaches, and emphasizes its technology rather than emphasizing that new practitioners must develop healthy therapeutic relationships. One way to do this is by entering counseling. We require all of our graduate students to participate in counseling as clients before they can begin their internship. The therapeutic relationship offered by their Christian counselor can be a model for their later relationships with their clients.

I started to help Charlie by making myself available for a healthy, trustworthy, and loving relationship. I began by carefully and respectfully listening to him. The initial interview was a two-hour session during which I took careful notes and asked Charlie to help me understand his story. I use a structured interview format so I am sure to not miss anything that may be important. The last question is, "To whom do you turn for emotional support?" We all need emotional support; our brains were designed for relationship with others. Many people who are struggling will respond with confusion, "Emotional support? No one really. My dog, I guess." In contrast, those who are resilient and handling their trauma well will usually list several people. About a third of the people I interview will include God in their response.

Charlie's response to the last question of the interview was, "Well, my partner, but he's retiring, so I don't really know. My wife, maybe, but I don't know anymore. She's so wrapped up in the girls. We just don't talk like we used to."

Brain-based Christian counseling (BBCC) begins with a follow-up to Charlie's response to my last question.

"Where are you with God?"

"Well, I guess I believe in God, but I haven't been going to church recently because I'm starting to wonder, and I just don't see the point. Honestly, I started asking myself that if there really is a God, why does he let things like this happen? This bad guy was really warped, and he hurt a lot of people; why did God let that happen?"

BBCC works to reestablish vertical, horizontal, and social brain integration. Optimally, we begin with vertical integration with God, but that's not always possible, and we have to start elsewhere. That was the case with Charlie. I admitted to Charlie that I didn't have an answer about why God let bad things like that happen, and we moved on, postponing the work I knew we eventually would need to do to reestablish his relationship with God.

Education about what was going on in his brain was important for Charlie. Many people seem to become more hopeful as they begin to understand that what they're experiencing has a physiological and neurological basis. I explained to Charlie that his fight-or-flight response had become chronically hyperaroused. I described how his *amygdala* and *hippocampus* could work better with his *cerebral cortex* to learn to discern threats so he could properly manage his emotional responses. I introduced this information gradually, responding to his questions and curiosity.

I used cognitive behavior therapy with a combination of systematic desensitization (SD) and personal prayer relaxation (PPR) to help Charlie begin to manage his hyperarousal. SD and PPR are often used together; progressive relaxation is part of both techniques.

Systematic desensitization starts with identifying the cause of the trauma and developing a hierarchy of thoughts about the trauma from least to most distressing. As therapy gets under way, we start with the least distressing thought and slowly progress up the hierarchy, gradually defusing the thought from its original emotional reaction by intervening with a relaxation response.

For Charlie, the imagined threat that the perpetrator could harm his daughters without his ability to protect them was at the core of his disorder. Do you remember that the young woman victim he had interviewed reminded him of his oldest daughter? Charlie had empathized with her husband and imagined watching her being raped and shot after he had been shot and disabled, an intrusive memory about which he was almost constantly ruminating. We developed a hierarchy of scenarios involving the perpetrator and his threat to Charlie's family.

We practiced progressive muscle relaxation with deep breathing while Charlie sat comfortably in a recliner chair that I use for this purpose. I introduced him to the subjective units of distress scale (SUDS) you can find at www.faithfulbrain.com. This is a personally subjective scale anchored at 0 for full relaxation with no distress, almost ready to fall asleep, up to 100, "I'm so anxious and distressed that I can't stand it!" I asked Charlie to set 50 as the SUDS level that would require action on his part; below 50 would be tolerated without taking action. Seated in my recliner, taking action at SUDS = 50 was defined as raising his right hand's index finger to tell me to stop moving up the hierarchy. At that point, I would stop and give Charlie an opportunity to reestablish his relaxation to take the SUDS level down to 30, signaled by Charlie raising the index finger on his left hand. Charlie got used to managing his anxiety, reporting, "It's great how I can control it with my breathing! I'm not sure how it's going to work outside I can really feel it here."

Personal prayer relaxation was the same approach I used with Carol in chapter 3. Charlie's PPR word was "Sam," his childhood dog, a large mixed breed in whose company he felt completely safe, comfortable, and relaxed. I provided him with recorded instructions to be used at home. Charlie paired Sam with his exhalation as he practiced relaxation. I helped Charlie expand his recollection of Sam by engaging all sensory modalities. We also established a recalled memory of a safe place for him to be with Sam, which was lying with him under a tree in his backyard during summer vacation when he was eight.

To help Charlie with his physiological arousal, I explained how exercise and nutrition work with brain-restorative sleep to return the brain to optimal health and fitness. I encouraged Charlie to get back to surfing and add jogging on the beach. We reviewed Charlie's nutrition and identified his overuse of highly caffeinated beverages to help him maintain alertness and improve his attention. His schedule had been severely disrupted over the previous few months, requiring overuse of caffeine to handle double shifts and unexpected emergencies. I encouraged him to gradually cut back on caffeine and treat it with intention, timing its use like a medicine. We especially focused on limiting use of caffeine near bedtime so he could get into deep sleep more quickly.

At the start of our fourth session, with solid rapport having been established and Charlie beginning to make good progress, I asked him if he would be open to discussing with me his faith in God. I explained that our long-term resilience seems to be related to our ability to transcend our circumstances and have faith in God, or at least in something or somebody bigger than ourselves.[178-182] I used the example of the United States in the days following the Pearl Harbor attacks; people seemed to come together and develop confidence from their unity. Charlie understood this and offered another example. "It's just like being on the SWAT team. You have the confidence to do what you couldn't do alone because you know you're going to be taken care of by the guys there with you."

I asked Charlie if there had ever been a time when he felt safe with God.

"Well, when I was a kid, my mom would pray with me when I went to bed each night, and as she tucked me in, she always said, 'God loves you, and I do too.' I haven't thought about that for a long time. Probably the last time was at her funeral a couple of years ago. Those were good times."

"Are you ever aware of God these days?"

"Yeah, actually, I was kinda thinking about God on Friday when I went out surfing after work as that storm was coming up from Mexico. The waves were huge, and they were still not blown out because the wind was shifting. There were incredible clouds, and I just sat there on my board and started thinking about God and how this just didn't all happen by accident. I thought how I'm really blessed to have a great wife and daughters. I almost wanted to pray."

I asked Charlie to consider getting back into a relationship with God to work on his emotional resilience so he'd be able to better handle future traumatic experiences.

"What does God have to do with my resilience?"

"Well, healthy and trustworthy relationships seem to be a key to resilience, like your being on the SWAT team. Our brains are designed to do best when we're in loving and trusting relationships with others. We handle stress better, we're less susceptible to infections and disease, and we recover from trauma better. And many people find that the most loving and trusting relationship they can have is with God. That's something I'd like you to explore because I've seen it help a lot of other people, including myself. I can't find a more safe and trusting relationship than my relationship with God."

There's a lot more to Charlie's story than we can cover here, but he did very well. After his daughters left home, he worked until his planned retirement, and he and his wife moved to a rural state. He went back to work in law enforcement, responsible for safety officers in a school district. He continued to develop his faith, which also became an important part of his relationship with his wife.

As I will describe throughout this book, optimal physical, mental, and cognitive health is the natural result of a faithful brain. To live life to the full, we must use our brain as God intended, indicated by its design and in a loving and trusting relationship with him. To borrow a phrase from an author who objects to the consilience of faith and science,[183] this is truly an *astonishing hypothesis*!

Chapter Takeaways

1. Thoughts and emotions are intertwined in the human brain.
2. A message cannot be fully comprehended independent of its emotional salience.
3. Faithful brain development depends on our relationship with Jesus.

4. The meaning of the Bible is enhanced through our relationship with Jesus.
5. Our relationships with other Christians increase the emotional salience of the Bible.

Discussion Questions

1. Go to the Vimeo link about Charlie at www.faithfulbrain.com and compare how you and he handle trauma.
2. How can you use your new understanding of emotional salience to experience Scripture and your faith more deeply?
3. How does your relationship with Jesus affect your understanding of the Bible?
4. When you study the Bible, what is the proportion of engagement between the right and left hemispheres of your brain, as depicted in figure 3? 50/50? 30/70? 90/10?
5. How might you achieve better balance between your hemispheres and experience the Bible more fully?
6. Share with another person your Faithful Brain Fitness report. Can you commit to improving your fitness over the next month?

CHAPTER 5

A Faithful Brain Is God-Rehabilitated

> Do not conform to the pattern of this world, but be transformed by the renewing of your mind. Then you will be able to test and approve what God's will is—his good, pleasing and perfect will.
> —*Romans 12:2*

Brain Basics

1. The careful study of people with brain injuries led to the development of neuroscience.
2. Personality and character are centered in the front of the cerebral cortex.
3. The ability to speak is centered in Broca's area in the left frontal cortex.
4. The ability to understand speech is centered in Wernicke's area in the left temporal lobe.
5. Neuroplasticity was described by the apostle Paul in the first century and named by William James in 1887 but not accepted as a scientific fact until the 1990s.

Leonard Matheson

What Is a God-Rehabilitated Brain?

The apostle Paul urged his followers to turn away from the world and turn toward God. To transform your mind, you must make your brain available to God so that neuroplasticity, neurogenesis, and neural epigenesis can help you become "God-rehabilitated." Your brain will be changed by these processes, which you might think of as being rewired.

The mistake many of us make is trying to be the agent of change, which is not what Paul wrote. The biblical narrative is that we must surrender and "be transformed" rather than transform ourselves. Surrender means we allow God to guide us, we trust God and make ourselves available for transformation. God is the agent of change, implemented through a relationship with Jesus.

In the Recovery community, you will often hear, "The door to Hell opens only from the inside." Surrender means we must open the door and invite God into our lives. Recovery begins after we open the door and look out into the light of truth, which feels painfully bright until we settle into trusting God's love and healing grace.

Paul tells us that the purpose for the transformation of our mind is to follow "God's perfect will." If we can accept that we exist in God's creation, it makes sense that we function best when we're in alignment with God's created reality. Dallas Willard wrote, "Reality is what you can count on; it's what you run into when you're wrong."[184] Choices that ignore the reality God created tend to cause problems. Continuing with such choices brings about changes in the brain that make those choices easier. We may begin to get addicted to our will, our way.

Although Paul understood this truth more than 2,000 years ago, neuroscience was slow to accept the ability of a brain to change. When I began my career in neurorehabilitation in 1970, I was taught that whatever recovery from a brain injury or stroke a patient had within six months after the injury was as much as we could expect. At that time, the conventional "truth" was that early in childhood, our brains stopped growing beyond small changes that reflected learning and the development of new memories.

A few years later, this six-month window was revised to two years. But by 1993, a forty-six-year-old father with two young children was told he could continue to improve his injured brain's function for the rest of his life as long as he worked at it.

Advances in our knowledge of the brain have been made by a careful study of the behavior and reports of people who have experienced brain damage. As they participate in neurorehabilitation, we learn how their brains work and help them make the most with what they have left, which can be very impressive. Explanations for our patients' experiences are proposed by clinicians, explored by neuroscientists, and then tested by clinicians with clients and their families. The cooperative and reiterative nature of neuroscientific discovery is important to emphasize because each neuroscience team member needs the others.

Neuroscience now confirms that the apostle Paul was excatly right in his letter to the Romans. When we stop conforming to the pattern of this world and instead follow the model offered by Jesus, our brain is rehabilitated and our mind is renewed. God transforms our emotions, thoughts, and behaviors.

Although I am delighted that neuroscientific research has confirmed Paul's wisdom about the underlying capacities of neuroplasticity, neurogenesis, and neural epigenesis, I am dismayed that it has taken so long. Many people could have been helped and lives saved if twentieth-century neuroscientists hadn't ignored the Bible and people of faith hadn't turned their backs on neuroscience. The slow pace of change in neurorehabilitation is a sad story I want to share with you now.

Who Was the First Brain Injury Patient?

On September 13, 1847, Phineas Gage, a well-respected and hard-working twenty-five-year-old American construction foreman, was blasting stone to clear a roadbed for the Rutland and Burlington Railroad. As he was tamping explosive powder into a hole he had drilled in solid rock, a spark ignited the powder and blew the tamping iron out of the hole, up into his left cheek, and through the top of his skull!

FIGURE 4.
PHINEAS GAGE

More than three and a half feet long and an inch and a quarter in diameter, the thirteen-pound iron rod landed a hundred feet away. It left a gaping hole from his face and left eye socket and up through the top of his head, along with massive destruction in the front of the cerebral cortex (the wrinkled covering) of his brain.

Amazingly, Gage was not killed. He was mostly blind in his left eye but remained conscious. Doctors patched him up as best they could, without benefit of anything more than scalpel, gauze, thread, and a sewing needle. Ether and aspirin hadn't been invented yet.

Gage took a few days off from work.

No, I just made up that last part! But it's true that after a few months of simple but careful medical care, Gage was in pretty good shape. He not only survived, he also became famous as a subject in medical science as well as an attraction in circus sideshows.

Gage lived for another thirteen years in good physical health, but he experienced major changes in his personality. Whereas before he had been friendly, gregarious, and easy to get along with, he became surly, angry, disrespectful, profane, impulsive, and unreliable.

It was from Gage that we learned that the forward and middle portions of the brain's frontal cortex (the prefrontal cortex) were crucial for personality, character, and self-control. Gage had lost major segments of what's now known as the ventromedial prefrontal cortex (VMPFC), with greater damage to the left hemisphere of his brain.[185] Although he could still reason, remember, and learn, his character had changed. It was said, "Gage was no longer Gage".

The year after Gage died in 1860, French anatomist Pierre Paul Broca discovered a small lesion on the left hemisphere of the cerebral cortex of one of his patients. The damaged area was at the back of the frontal lobe, just behind the area that had been damaged in Gage's brain.

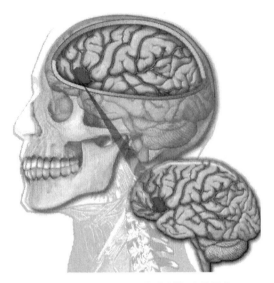

FIGURE 5. BROCA'S AREA

Broca called this man "Tan," because he was able to articulate only one sound, "tan" although he could understand perfectly everything spoken to him. How are you? "Tan." Did you have a nice sleep? "Tan." What's the weather outside? "Tan." What's your mother's name? "Tan."

Broca deduced that this damaged area of the left frontal cortex was responsible for the man's loss of the ability to speak, which we now call Broca's Area. It was from Broca and Tan that we began to appreciate that the left hemisphere of the brain is responsible for speech in most people.

Fifteen years later, in 1876, Polish anatomist Carl Wernicke identified another area on the left cerebral cortex a few inches behind and below Broca's Area that when damaged interfered with the ability to understand speech. If this area was damaged and Broca's area was healthy, people were able to form words and sentences and speak so they could be understood, but they could not understand what was said to them.

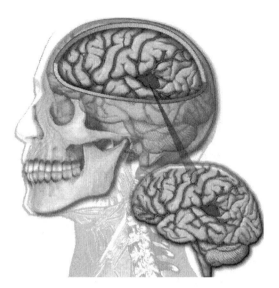

FIGURE 6. WERNICKE'S AREA

Wernicke would ask, "What's the weather look like today?" The patient would respond, "It's good to see you, too" or "I'm feeling just fine, thanks" or "I'd like milk with my tea, please."

People with damage to this area of the left temporal lobe are able to hear your words just fine but struggle to understand what is said. They try to figure out what you're saying by the context, and they see by the look on your face that their response is off target, but they can't do anything about it. People with damage to what he called Wernicke's Area just don't understand what they're hearing.

Hey! Let's all name brain areas after each other.

Actually, Korbinian Brodmann beat us to the punch. He named fifty-two Brodmann Areas in 1909.[186] Even today, many scientific studies refer to BA 13 or BA 34 to describe regions of the brain.

Broca, Wernicke, and Brodmann had identified different areas in the brain that were responsible for different functions. Over the next several years, many others who studied the anatomy of the brain (called neuroanatomists) confirmed that these areas control the same functions in all humans, which was a very exciting idea. The simplicity of the idea that the brain was hard wired was very appealing. Neuroanatomists started to publish brain maps based on thousands of anatomical studies of the brains of people who had experienced strokes and other brain injuries.

After death, the limitations of these people that appeared when their brains were damaged could be traced by autopsy to particular areas of damage. In this way, neuroanatomists and neuropsychologists could fairly well predict what part of the brain was responsible for a certain function or ability. Each person's brain appeared quite similar and functioned in similar ways, so that injuries to the same area always led to the same limitations. Neuroanatomists thought they finally understood how the brain worked!

In 1913, Spanish neuroanatomist Santiago Ramón y Cajal reported that the pathways in the adult brain are "fixed, ended, and immutable."[187] He won a Nobel Prize for this, and it was accepted as truth for the next several decades.

As it turned out, things were not so simple. Throughout this book, we will find that God-wired brains are much more complex and dynamic than were ever imagined by the early brain mappers.

When Did the Idea of Neuroplasticity Arise?

Even though static brain maps were exciting, in 1887, American psychologist William James had introduced the idea of neuroplasticity. James reported that "organic matter, especially nervous tissue, seems endowed with a very extraordinary degree of plasticity ... a structure weak enough to yield to influence."[188]

James was the first to describe what we now know as neuroplasticity. He described the ability of the brain to become rewired so that if a part of the brain that was originally responsible for a certain ability or function was damaged, another part of the brain could be trained to take over.

In 1949, Canadian psychologist Donald O. Hebb proposed a model that explained how neuroplasticity occurred: Change actually takes place in the linkages among the neurons that are involved. Hebb borrowed a phrase for which he has become famous: "Cells that fire together wire together."[22] This describes the strengthening of neural linkages that occur with practice.

Unfortunately, the ideas of James and Hebb were mostly ignored late into the twentieth century. The simplistic brain maps were joined by simple human behavior models of psychologists such as John Watson and B. F. Skinner, which would dominate psychology and brain science for several decades.

In spite of what was being taught in the best universities and medical schools, the hard wiring of brains was not what we found in 1970 in the neurorehabilitation of Peter and others who had brain damage at Rancho Los Amigos. Every day, we saw clear evidence of the benefits of harnessing their brain's neuroplasticity.

We had substantial success rehabilitating people who had experienced brain injuries from accidents and strokes through our

> **Just-Right Challenge**
> When the demands of a meaningful task slightly exceed ability, harnessing neuroplasticity.

persistent use of *just-right challenges*. A just-right challenge occurs when the demands of a meaningful task slightly exceed the client's ability. As you read in chapter 1, we helped Peter by providing him with a task that slightly exceeded his ability. We had no neuroscience to support us back then, but this approach definitely helped people improve. We now understand that just-right challenges stimulate and harness the brain's neuroplasticity.

But neuroscience had not caught up with what a few clinicians had found were reasonable expectations for brain rehabilitation..[189-192] Neuroscience still had about three decades to go.

In the late 1970s, American psychologist Edward Taub surgically cut the nerves that supplied sensation to one hand of macaque monkeys and then allowed the monkeys to remain in their cages or forced them to use the non-feeling hands to feed themselves. He found that the monkeys abandoned use of the non-feeling hands unless they were forced to use them.[193] Taub's methods were so controversial that he became the first target of the PETA animal rights movement, which effectively shut down his research and confiscated his animals in 1981. Although he was eventually cleared of wrongdoing, he was severely castigated and had his career sidelined for many years.

In 1983, two American psychologists, Michael Merzenich and Jon Kaas, published research[194] that described how what you do gradually changes brain wiring. They severed a nerve in a monkey's hand that provided sensory signals from the third finger of the hand to the brain and studied the effect of the absent signal on the monkey's brain. Without a signal from the third finger, that part of the brain should have been silent because it was not being stimulated. However, they found that the brain region rewired itself to process signals from other parts of the monkey's hand. Because the third finger's brain-geography wasn't being used, it was recruited to help out with other tasks so the second and fourth fingers became more broadly represented on the sensory cortex.

When Merzenich and Kaas attempted to publish their studies, they met with resistance and rejection. The conventional wisdom was that if neuroplasticity were real, the brain would become disorganized and chaotic. The apostle Paul's encouragement to transform our mind and William James's description of nervous tissue's plasticity had been forgotten or ignored.

Fortunately, Merzenich and Kaas persisted and extended their neuroplasticity model to demonstrate that repetitive behavior changed the brain.[195-197] Practicing a task for several hours each day led to larger areas of the brain being responsible for that skill.[197-200] For example, a violinist's practice with the fingering hand leads to growth of the fingering area in the brain for that hand but not for the other hand, because the hand that holds the bow doesn't do much fingering.[37]

Another interesting series of studies on the neuroplasticity of the adult brain involves London taxicab drivers.[201] For them to become licensed, they have to master a demanding series of lessons and tests that involve every intersection in London. Over several years, the driver must learn what they refer to as "The Knowledge." MRI studies of the brains of these drivers have demonstrated a much larger right hippocampus (where directional memories originate) than their left hippocampus. [201] Even more interesting, the right hippocampus of the taxi drivers was larger than that of bus drivers,[202] probably because the latter follow fixed routes. Learning complex routes harnessed neuroplasticity to increase millions of new links among neurons! Requiring taxicab drivers to learn The

Knowledge required thousands of just-right challenges that stimulated neuroplasticity and neurogenesis.

How Did Neurorehabilitation Develop?

Neurorehabilitation began as treatment for people with brain injuries in the late 1800s and advanced rapidly in each major war as combat veterans made urgent demands on health care. But even with the courageous pioneering of some very creative people, we're still not very far along. Although we continue to be hopeful, none of my colleagues are satisfied with our progress.

One of the most exciting stories in neurorehabilitation involved the Bach-y-Rita family, Paul and his brother George. In 1958, their father, Pedro, a New York poet and college professor, experienced a severe stroke that paralyzed the right side of his body and made him unable to speak. George was a medical student who moved his father into his home and encouraged him to do as much on his own as he could. For example, every day for months, Pedro sat in the garden, trying to pull weeds with his non-functional right hand. George and his roommates worked with Pedro several hours each day, practicing basic activities such as washing his face and dressing.

Over several months of intense repetition, Pedro gradually improved. Two years later he was able to return to work as a college professor. He died of a heart attack five years after that while he was on a hike in the Andes. A brain autopsy found that the earlier stroke had destroyed 95% of the brain tissue that should have been required to do all that he had done!

Pedro's amazing recovery encouraged Paul to spend the rest of his life applying neuroscience to rehabilitation. His pioneering work in the use of neuroplasticity has helped to establish our knowledge of the long-term ability of the damaged brain to benefit from just-right challenges so that function can be restored.[203-207] This has been applied to several exciting innovations, including those that help blind people learn to see through their tongue rather than their eyes.[203] There are wonderful YouTube videos available that describe their work with people who are blind, including a blind mountain-climber!

Although we now know that the hardwired neuroanatomical approach to the brain is much too narrow, American health care continues to be limited by this thinking. Only in the past few years has the constraint-induced movement therapy proposed many years ago by Taub[208-210] become available as an evidence-based intervention. The unfortunate delay has meant that millions of people have had incomplete rehabilitation. Even today, authorization by insurance carriers for rehabilitation to fully harness neuroplasticity is rare; most Americans who experience brain injury or stroke receive only a few months of part-time rehabilitation, leaving them far short of their neurorehabilitation potential. If you're wealthy or have strong political connections, the full extent of neurorehabilitation is available. Otherwise, neurorehabilitation services are very limited.

> **Constraint-Induced Movement Therapy**
> Stimulating neuroplasticity to migrate control in the brain of a paralyzed arm by restricting use of the "good" hand.

I encourage families with loved ones who experience stroke or brain injury or cerebral palsy to investigate this research and seek professional guidance to implement neurorehabilitation such as constraint-induced movement (CIM) therapy, even if it's not authorized by insurance. Much can be done by family members, such as the Bach-y-Rita family did for Pedro. This is especially important for children.[211-213] If you can't find a physician who is knowledgeable about CIM or hippotherapy and other modern neurorehabilitation services, you can hire an occupational therapist or physical therapist privately to work with you in your home.[213] Properly trained occupational therapists, physical therapists, rehabilitation psychologists, neurologists, and rehabilitation medicine physicians can help you and your family harness the brain processes that neuroscience has identified.

Should the Bible Inform Science?

The conventional wisdom in scientific circles is "Of course not!" Using the Bible to inform science is considered fuzzy, uninformed, and unprofessional. For the first half of my career, I agreed, but over the last twenty-five years, I have changed my opinion. Researching this book has moved me to argue that the Bible should be part of medical scientists' undergraduate education. For clinicians, Bible illiteracy creates problems when they work with clients who know more than the clinicians do about the Bible. For researchers, the Bible can be orienting and encouraging, as it could have been in the example of neuroplasticity. We needed biblically literate scientists to come to the defense of pioneering neuroscientists such as Edward Taub, Michael Merzenich, and Jon Kaas. Their political enemies, sometimes supported by traditional religious zealots with an anti-scientific bias, seriously slowed the development of neurorehabilitation.

The downside potential of the separation of faith and science is clear in the history of resistance to the reality of neuroplasticity. If twentieth-century scientists had seriously considered Paul's first-century letter to the Romans as inspired insight into the design of our brain, the antipathy toward neuroplasticity might have evaporated decades earlier than it did. The appointment of Francis Collins, a born-again Christian, as the director of the National Institutes of Health, the world's largest research institution, the launch of two scientific journals focused on faith and religion by the American Psychological Association, and its publication of the *Handbook of Psychology, Religion, and Spirituality* [214, 215] help me be optimistic about the developing integration of faith and science. As the editors of the *Handbook* report,

> In the past 20 years, the psychology of religion and spirituality has opened up to a host of new topics-virtues, attachment, coping, meaning-making, modeling, struggles, evil, meditation, relational spirituality, and spiritually integrated interventions, to name just a few. The findings from these studies clarify that religion and spirituality can be potent resources for many people or sources of stress in and of themselves.
> ([214] page 8)

Fair and balanced scientific examination of faith, religious practices, and spiritual experiences is important and exciting because it deals with intimate topics that have lifelong personal relevance. Indeed, most of the world's religions argue that this relevance extends into eternity. Without good scientific research, we're left with polemic diatribes such as *God Is Not Great: How Religion Poisons Everything*[216] and *The God Delusion*,[217] worldwide bestsellers that are either actively ignored by communities of faith or ineffectively attacked with zeal that lacks an objective foundation, such as you're learning now.

I agree that the Bible is not a science text, but as you have seen with the apostle Paul's anticipation of the science of neuroplasticity, and as you will see in the next chapter on the science of love, it's a substantial repository of inspired knowledge and wisdom. People of faith who become engaged in the scientific enterprise will grow their faith toward the unlimited nature of God.

Beyond its importance to the individual, engagement of people of faith in the scientific enterprise will improve synchrony with God's created reality, thereby facilitating more-rapid discoveries of knowledge. I strongly encourage people of faith to volunteer for an institutional review board (IRB) in their communities. Usually centered in universities and hospitals, IRBs provide oversight of the ethical treatment of subjects in scientific research. Developed in response to the horrors of Nazi research on humans and the American Tuskegee Syphilis Study, the IRB reviews the protection of the rights of research subjects.[218] Each IRB is required to have at least one member who represents a religious or faith-based organization and at least one independent citizen, thereby providing a forum for communication. I have participated in hundreds of such committees and usually find them to be exemplary experiences.

By the way, the forty-six-year-old father with two young children who was told in 1993 he could continue to improve the function of his injured brain for the rest of his life as long as he worked at it, was me. I sustained a concussion when thrown from a horse. My "mild traumatic brain injury" created problems with cognitively complex tasks. I was prescribed neurorehabilitation activities that I adopted with gusto. Over the next few years, I restored my ability to handle complex tasks. I have continued to challenge myself so that today I am "smarter" than I was before the concussion. I am a believer in the methods I use to guide my clients because I have experienced their benefits myself.

Chapter Takeaways

1. The careful study of people with brain injuries has led the development of neuroscience.
2. Personality and character are centered in the front of the cerebral cortex.
3. The phenomenon of neuroplasticity was acknowledged by the apostle Paul in the first century and named by William James in 1887.
4. Neuroplasticity was not accepted as a scientific fact until the 1990s and was not part of evidence-based medicine until the last few years.
5. The inspired knowledge and wisdom of the Bible can be helpful to neuroscientists.

Discussion Questions

1. What is the connection between "God's perfect will" and your life to the full?
2. How often do you select just-right challenges to develop your brain?
3. What can you do to encourage your doctors and other caregivers to integrate your faith into their care for you and your family?
4. Would you be open to serving on an institutional review board as a lay member to review scientific research and the protection of research subjects?

CHAPTER 6

A Faithful Brain Is Heart Balanced

> It is I, the Eternal One, who probes the innermost heart and examines the innermost thoughts.
> —*Jeremiah 17:10*

Brain Basics

1. Your brain and heart are vertically integrated.
2. Thoughts originating in your brain are communicated by the vagus nerve to your heart.
3. Responses of your heart are communicated by the vagus nerve to your brain.
4. Vagus nerve tone is crucial to healthy heart-brain balance.
5. Moral uncertainty disrupts heart function.

Does My Heart Think?

The Bible verse that introduces this chapter is the modern version of Jeremiah 17:10. The ancient Hebrew version described God as probing the heart *and* kidneys! What's that about? Actually, we think with our whole being, including our heart and kidneys![6] Modern people often make the mistake of believing our thoughts occur only in the brain. While it's true that our brain is at the center of our nervous system, it's fully integrated with our body, especially our heart.

The Bible points to the importance of the heart as compared with the mind; "heart" appears 833 times in the King James Bible, while "mind" appears only 95 times. We should take this as a clue; our heart is very important to God, and caring for our body is a spiritual responsibility. Proper nutrition, exercise, and sleep help us feel better and think more clearly, because our brain is integrated with our body.

Neuroscience supports that your heart and your brain are intimately and purposely connected. Your heart and brain influence each other reciprocally to help maintain emotional and physiological balance. Links between our brain and heart are interactive, providing two-way communication. This helps the heart participate with the brain in guiding our lives. One way to look at this is that your heart helps your brain think.

"Nobody believes me! I'm not faking!"

Judy was a patient at the Rancho Pediatrics Pavilion a few months after Peter was discharged. She was a smart and stylish sixteen-year-old high school sophomore who was entirely normal except for one big exception—Judy had grand mal seizures but didn't have epilepsy. Judy had a psychogenic nonepileptic seizure (PNES) disorder. Approximately 1 in 50,000 people has the very rare PNES disorder, which is much less common than an epileptic seizure disorder. Although her seizures looked exactly like grand mal epileptic seizures created by electrical chaos in her brain, Judy's

---

[6] The kidneys manufacture epinephrine, norepinephrine, and cortisol.

brain was entirely normal during a seizure. All the experts were consulted and all the medicines were tried without any benefit; she continued to have two or three seizures every day. Judy puzzled us all.

Some people thought that Judy was a malingerer, that she was faking her seizures. But this didn't make sense because the seizures were interfering with the life she loved. They stopped her from going to high school, where she was popular and a good student. They frightened her family and girlfriends, with whom she had great relationships. They threatened her relationship with her boyfriend, who was afraid to be alone with her. Worst of all, Judy couldn't get her driver's license, a big deal for a teenager in Los Angeles. People with seizures aren't allowed to drive. I didn't know what to make of Judy; I was completely puzzled.

I was talking with Judy one afternoon on the patio outside her hospital room when her eyes rolled back and her body stiffened. She slid from her chair to the ground, convulsing violently. The nurses and pediatrician were there almost immediately and checked her out while I stood by. They decided to give her privacy and make her safe and comfortable and let the seizure pass. They asked me to stay with her. I sat quietly on the ground next to her as she convulsed and writhed. Partitions were brought over to give us privacy. But someone else snuck in.

I guess I should say "someone" because Clowny was not only a dog; she was a member of the Rancho Pediatrics family. In fact, she was the most popular member of our family, the only pet allowed in the hospital. Clowny came over to Judy, sniffed her a few times, and nuzzled and licked her hand. Judy's hand and body immediately writhed toward Clowny, she took a very deep breath, and as she exhaled, the seizure gradually subsided.

Wow! I was surprised and worried by what I had just witnessed. If it had been an epileptic grand mal seizure, Judy should not have been able to respond to Clowny.[219] Clowny sat back, and we looked at each other. I must have had a puzzled look on my face; was that a wise smile or a smirk on Clowny's muzzle? Maybe Judy *was* faking! Either that, or something was badly out of balance.

How Had Judy Gotten So Badly out of Balance?

Before we understood about the importance of brain integration, people believed that emotions were situated in the body and didn't involve the brain. Because love and desire are felt in our heart, and fear is felt in our gut, and happiness fully engages our face and eyes, it was assumed that those spots were where each of these feelings resided.

In fact, I still have clients warn me, "Don't you dare tell me this is 'all in my head.' I know what I feel!" I often counter this by offering examples of clients with phantom pain after a limb amputation and compare their experience to clients with complete spinal cord injuries who have intact physical bodies without sensation. This comparison helps explain that our body is experienced only in our brain. We are designed to be fully integrated beings.

Peoples' belief that emotions do not involve the brain is an example of brain dis-integration we explored in chapter 3 and runs counter to how we were designed. It wasn't until late in the nineteenth century that body-brain integration became a focus of research.

In 1884, William James, the founder of American psychology, reported, "The emotional-brain-processes not only resemble the ordinary sensorial brain-processes, but in very truth are nothing but such processes variously combined."[[220]] page 188) His point was that emotions arise elsewhere but awareness of them occurs in the brain. The brain is where we become aware of sensations such as touch and pain as well as emotions such as love and fear.

In 1914, Walter Cannon, a Harvard physician and physiologist, described the balanced design of the nerves involved with emotional processing.[[221]] He described separate divisions of the nervous system that innervated the body, one that excited and another that calmed. He reported that nerve endings at each of the organs tend to be antagonistic to each other, to either excite or calm our organs and provide balance. This is known as the autonomic nervous system (ANS). It's called autonomic because it's automatic, operating in the background without our direct control. The ANS is composed of two primary branches, the sympathetic nervous system (SNS), which excites, and the parasympathetic nervous system (PNS), which calms. In healthy humans, these maintain physiological and emotional balance.[[222]]

Cannon expanded his ideas in a landmark book in 1932, *The Wisdom of the Body*,[[223]] in which he popularized the idea of

Homeostasis

The automatic balancing of bodily processes.

homeostasis. This is a complex set of automatic processes that constantly monitor and adjust systems in your brain and body to maintain physiologic stability and to support emotional balance. Homeostasis depends on communication of the brain among the viscera, muscles, and blood vessels. Your body's ability to maintain your temperature at 98.6 degrees Fahrenheit and your blood sugar and blood oxygen/carbon dioxide at optimal levels are examples of homeostasis.

Cannon explained that our emotional processing occurs in the brain's *limbic system*, beneath the cerebral cortex.[224] The limbic system vertically integrates the cerebral cortex with emotions throughout our bodies. This is where sensory messages are first received in the brain and where emotional responses originate, triggering changes throughout the brain and body that we later interpret as fear, rage, love, sadness, and so forth.

Let's take a closer look at the limbic system, which is found in each cerebral hemisphere. The *thalamus* and *amygdala* are among the earliest brain structures to develop, which gives a baby awareness of incoming sensory information before she is able to process it fully. Babies react emotionally, with the ability to understand developing later, during the first few years. The thalamus and amygdala are closely linked to the *hippocampus*, which matures more slowly and continues to develop over the lifespan. It's one of the few brain structures to grow throughout adulthood, regenerating itself constantly.

Your thalamus is the central relay station for most of your sensory data. Everything your body senses, other than smell, is routed through your thalamus and transmitted elsewhere.

Your amygdala is the centerpiece of your threat-detection system, always ready to trigger a response to a threat. Sensory information coming through the thalamus is constantly monitored by your amygdala. If your amygdala detects a threat or challenge, it immediately and automatically mobilizes your threat-response system.

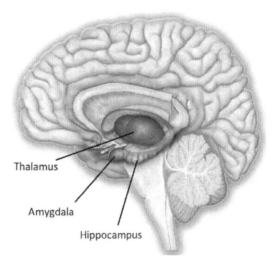

FIGURE 7. KEY ELEMENTS OF THE LIMBIC SYSTEM

The hippocampus helps you learn to discern real threats from apparent threats that don't require a response, all based on prior experiences. It works with your cerebral cortex to develop your ability to identify the threat or challenge and take proper action, modulating your threat-response system. In counseling, when we help people discern real from imagined threats, we're working with their cerebral cortex and hippocampus, developing neural patterns that differentiate, for instance, a garter snake from a rattlesnake.

Together, the thalamus, amygdala, and hippocampus make up a detection and response system that's constantly surveying your environment to identify potential threats and challenges. This system automatically triggers very strong automatic reactions to threats and challenges, what Cannon called your "fight or flight response." It causes you either to stand your ground and fight or flee to safety.

If you're walking in the woods and hear a rattle or rustle, the thalamus receives the signal and passes it to the amygdala, which interprets the sound as a threat because your brain has what's known as a "negative response bias." Because of this bias, the amygdala automatically triggers defensive action and causes your hippocampus and cerebral cortex to try to discern whether the sound was the rattle of a snake or the rustle of oak leaves. At the same time, the thalamus has sent the message to other brain and body structures. These brain structures (hypothalamus, pituitary gland, and adrenal glands) automatically release powerful brain chemicals to support and guide your ability to respond to the threat or challenge.

Your brain is designed so that the thalamus and amygdala trigger the response twenty-five to one-hundred milliseconds *before* your cerebral cortex becomes aware of the threat or challenge. Your body's response has already started by the time you become aware that you have been threatened or challenged. Your cerebral cortex then works with your hippocampus to catch up and try to make sense of what triggered the alarm and what you should do next. If the sound was a rattle of a snake, you take different action than if it was the rustling of leaves.

Cannon pointed out that we must cognitively interpret our emotional responses, and he offered a great example: The responses of the heart and most other organs during both fear and rage are identical even though we perceive them as totally opposite emotions.

Cannon focused on the limbic system and how it created our emotional responses, but he didn't study how thinking could affect our emotional responses. That work was begun in the 1960s by Aaron Beck, a psychoanalyst who was dissatisfied with Sigmund Freud's ideas about the cause of depression. [225] Beck noticed that his patients' emotional responses were caused by "automatic thoughts."

depressive's perseverating self-blame
self-criticism appear to be related to
centric notions of causality and his
penchant for criticizing himself for his alleged deficiencies. He is particularly prone to ascribe adverse occurrences to some deficiency in himself and then to rebuke himself for having this alleged defect. In the more severe cases, the patient may blame himself for happenings that are in no way connected with him and abuse himself in a savage manner. Eighty percent of the severely depressed patients reported this symptom.[225] page 24)

Beck argued that habitual thoughts contributed to depression and anxiety disorders. People got into habits of interpreting threats and challenges in ways that created emotional imbalance and impeded homeostasis. Beck's approach to correcting the relationship between thoughts and emotions is called *cognitive behavior therapy* (CBT), shown by thousands of studies to be an effective approach to counseling for people with depression, anxiety, and many other disorders.

Because of its role in learning to discern, the hippocampus is an important focus of our efforts in counseling. Cognitive behavior therapy helps us clearly discern the threat or challenge, and these memories are stored away by the hippocampus. When a person has developed depression, post-traumatic stress disorder, anxiety disorders, and other problems to which stress contributes, counseling helps clarify the threat or challenge. Depending on how we interpret the threat or challenge, we can take proper action. As we take action, the limbic system calms and the body is able to return to homeostasis, with these memories stored by the hippocampus so we can discern a snake's rattle from the rustling of leaves more easily the next time.

How Does My Heart Help My Brain Think?

Vertical integration from the cerebral cortex to the limbic system extends down into the body along two major pathways, the brain stem going into the spinal cord, and the vagus nerve extending from the brain stem into the vagal nervous system. In separate research efforts, Steven Porges[89] and Julian Thayer[94] have taken somewhat different approaches to describe synchronization of the brain with the heart. Both models support the idea that our heart is involved with our thinking and our ability to process emotional responses.

Thayer's research focuses on how changes in the heart reflect and influence brain function. The number of milliseconds between each heartbeat will change, depending on what you're doing and how you're feeling. This change is called heart rate variability (HRV). What's very interesting is that HRV is closely related to emotional health. Depressed patients have low HRV, as do people with anxiety disorders, serious phobias, post-traumatic stress disorder, and schizophrenia.[94] For these people, the time between each heartbeat is very steady and doesn't change in response to changing circumstances; they have low HRV. In people who are emotionally healthy, HRV changes in response to changing circumstances; they have high HRV. When our HRV is high, we tend to be emotionally flexible, adaptive, and more emotionally resilient.

The Porges approach to the relationship between your heart and brain focuses on communication that occurs through the vagal nervous system based in large part on the from the heart through the vagal nervous system in.

Our *vagus nerve* starts in your brain stem as the tenth of twelve cranial nerves. Five of the cranial nerves work together in what Porges has called the "social engagement system," coordinating the face, middle-ear muscles, bronchi, heart, and vocal muscles.

The vagal nervous system is involved with the vertical integration of your brain and body as a key part of the parasympathetic branch of your autonomic nervous system (ANS). The vagal nervous system helps the ANS balance the sympathetic nervous system's fight-or-flight response. After the emergency has passed, homeostasis is restored to allow your body to replenish itself, often known as "rest and digest."[222]

Much of your ability to calm depends on a well-toned vagus nerve, as in muscles that are well-toned. People with poor vagus nerve tone are on-edge and easily frustrated and angry; they have more difficulty controlling their anger, experiencing it as spiraling up and out of control more often. People with good vagus nerve tone tend to calm quickly after a threat has passed and they get over their anger more quickly.[226] With a healthy and fit vagal nervous system,

1. You sleep better.[227]
2. Your brain can be calmed by a soothing voice.[228]
3. You are less likely to be clinically depressed.[229]
4. You are less likely to have a cardiac arrest.[229, 230]
5. Your metabolic and immune systems improve.[231]

Artificial vagus nerve stimulation can calm the brain directly. In 1997 the U.S. Food and Drug Administration (FDA) approved an electronic vagus nerve stimulator for epileptic seizure control.[232] Vagus nerve stimulation also improves mood, and the device was approved by the FDA for treatment of severe depression in 2005.

Although most of the links between your brain and body are transmitted through the spinal cord, important heart-to-brain communication travels through your vagus nerve. Because most (80 percent) of the vagal nervous system communication is up to the brain, it's crucial for providing the brain with information about heart function.

In addition to calming the ANS, the vagus nerve also affects heart rate variability. Both the calming effect on the ANS, and the emotional flexibility of high HRV are communicated between the heart and brain by the vagus nerve.

So when God looks into our heart and finds low HRV and up through the vagus nerve into the brain and finds us locked in anxious or angry or depressed thinking, something is wrong. As I look at this from a Christian counselor's perspective, it appears to me that the habitual thoughts that concerned Beck have replaced the experience of love and safety flowing out of our relationship with God. Calming our heart by relaxing in the safe love of God allows us to experience less anxiety.[222, 233-235]

This area of research is so new that only one peer-reviewed report has been published. In a 2014 study of African-American women,[91] the effects of prayer on their response to racism was examined. Prayer was found to improve their coping with racism and this was reflected in their increased HRV.

In addition to prayer, another application of these ideas is to improve HRV through biofeedback training, which I sometimes recommend to my clients. Training to improve HRV has been shown to improve emotional stability and physical health.[236-239] All these benefits appear to depend on a well-developed vagus nerve.

How Does Love Affect the Vagus Nerve?

Early love relationships influence the heart-brain link because the vagus nerve develops rapidly in the third trimester of pregnancy and over the first twelve months after birth.[90] You can see this in the startle response of the newborn that is gradually controlled under the stable influence of parents' love.

The vagal nervous system helps infants tune into mom's calming voice; it communicates its soothing effects throughout the body. Children who are severely neglected don't develop these self-soothing abilities. Even when they're well loved, the genetic absence of this ability, making them less responsive to soothing voices,[89, 90] may be one of the challenges facing children with autism.

Vagus nerve tone improves as you experience loving and trusting relationships,[240] while insecure relationships weaken your vagal tone. Fortunately, this is reversible, and when we speak of taking time for the "heart to heal," it's the vagal nervous system that needs to be returned to healthy tone so that the heart-brain connection can help put the person back into emotional balance. As creatures who were designed to be in loving relationships, loving touch is therapeutic for depression, anxiety, and overall mental health.[241] Measured in terms of heart rate variability, loving touch is therapeutic. Massage therapy is rapidly becoming a scientifically recognized intervention for numerous ailments.

One of the best-studied effects of loving touch is found in modern neonatal intensive care units, using an ancient strategy that's common in many undeveloped countries. Preterm infants are aided to develop good vagal nerve tone with kangaroo care (KC), a strategy to reduce neonatal morbidity and mortality.[242-244] As soon after birth as possible, the infant is placed in skin-to-skin contact on the mother's chest. In addition to tactile stimulation, the infant receives stimulation of the vestibular balance system in the inner ear from the movement of mother's breathing and auditory stimulation from mother's voice, breath sounds, and heartbeat. Research has demonstrated that KC provided by the father is also beneficial. Both kangaroo care and light tactile massage have been demonstrated to help infants more rapidly develop their vagal nervous system.[241] Improvements are seen in increased birth weight, more sound sleep, and more rapid emotional, physical, cognitive, and interpersonal development.

Why Are We Designed This Way?

Although neuroscience can only hint at answers to this question, we can find guidance in the Bible. In Genesis 2:16–17, we learn, "And the Lord God commanded the man, 'You are free to eat from any tree in the garden; but you must not eat from the tree of the knowledge of good and evil, for when you eat from it you will certainly die.'"

The biblical narrative describes Adam and Eve as disobeying God and eating the apple. I interpret this from a neuroscience perspective as trading the certainty of secure life with God for the freedom of an insecure life apart from God.

It's important to recognize that the choice to seek autonomy from God leads to dangerous uncertainty.[245] The focus of the biblical narrative on "the knowledge of good and evil" has to do with the ability to discern right from wrong and anticipate the outcomes of our everyday decisions. This knowledge is much more important than factual knowledge. Morality and ethics are types of uncertainty with dangerous consequences. When we are uncertain about morality, we create chaos for ourselves and others, much greater than when we are uncertain about facts. The effects of this type of uncertainty include deep anxiety that limits our ability to love and be lovable in secure relationships.

Our brains are designed to live and grow in the context of secure, loving relationships. Insecure attachment relationships are one of the results of turning away from God. I believe that this is why the vagal nervous system is designed to develop under the influence of love, and it can be rehabilitated with Jesus as a model for our interpersonal relationships. Being redeemed by Jesus is an intimate act, like kangaroo care for our soul. One of the results of redemption is that Jesus becomes our primary attachment figure, guiding the restoration of secure relationships with others. In these ways, God's love and the love of others can improve the vagal nervous system and our heart-brain link.

In my own life, my willfulness always creates uncertainty when I attempt to turn away from God. If this is inconsistent with God's design, I should expect that uncertainty would negatively affect my brain. And this is exactly what neuroscience has discovered; uncertainty detrimentally affects our brain in large part by its influence on our vagal nervous system.[94]

Although uncertainty should be neutral (something may or may not happen), humans have a built-in "negativity bias" that causes uncertainty to create anxiety.[246] Through the effects of anxiety, uncertainty damages our brain, vagal nervous system, heart, and body. The biblical narrative suggests to me that our sin creates uncertainty for which we were not designed. We need to be redeemed from our sin and rehabilitated from the effects of our uncertainty.

Faith in God's trustworthy love and grace delivers us from uncertainty. I am dependably rescued from the pain of uncertainty by the grace of God, calming my anxiety. As I meditate on God's certain love that replaces my ruminations on the uncertainty of life, my anxiety recedes. As my pastor says, "If you know how to worry, you also know how to meditate on Scripture."[247]

For me, the ultimate healing of my damaged heart-brain links and resolution of my many insecure attachments began by inviting God into my life. Early in the development of my faith, the Third-Step Prayer of Dr. Bob, a founder of Alcoholics Anonymous, helped me get started.

> Dear God, I'm sorry about the mess I've made of my life. I want to turn away from all the wrong things I've ever done and all the wrong things I've ever been. Please forgive me for it all. I know You have the power to change my life and can turn me into a winner. Thank You, God for getting my attention long enough to interest me in trying it Your way.
>
> God, please take over the management of my life and everything about me. I am making this conscious decision to turn my will and my life over to Your care and am asking You to please take over all parts of my life.
>
> Please, God, move into my heart. However You do it is Your business, but make Yourself real inside me and fill my awful emptiness. Fill me

> with your love and Holy Spirit and make me know Your will for me. And now, God, help Yourself to me and keep on doing it. I'm not sure I want You to, but do it anyhow.
>
> I rejoice that I am now a part of Your people, that my uncertainty is gone forever, and that You now have control of my will and my life. Thank You and I praise Your name.

Because I am a willful person, I had to pray this prayer and others like it often, some days many times, especially "I'm not sure I want You to, but do it anyhow."

After accepting the gift of redemption from Jesus on August 3, 1995, I find myself more easily relaxing in God's certain love. Redemption paved the way for my personal neurorehabilitation that continues today, even as I write these words. If you haven't yet accepted Jesus' gift of a secure love relationship with God, won't you consider joining me?

What Happened to Judy?

Although we had very little neuroscience to guide us in 1971, I now realize that our approach to Judy took advantage of her heart-brain link. She has become an important example to me of how love helps to develop a faithful brain. Starting with Clowny's nuzzling, the loving care we offered gradually diminished her autonomic hyperarousal in part by balancing her autonomic nervous system through strengthening her vagus nerve. We now have evidence-based therapies for people with psychogenic non-epileptic seizure disorders, but I always remind myself that we were successful with Judy because we cared for her with love. With the benefit of four decades of neuroscientific research, I now understand how love affects our vagal nervous system[248] and thereby our brain and heart. [177] Her parents, nurses, doctors, therapists, teachers, and even her headstrong twenty-four-year-old counselor tapped into the heart-based healing power of love in Judy's brain and heart linked through her vagal nervous system.

As the frequency of her seizures began to abate, when summer vacation came, Judy was transferred to Casa Consuelo, Rancho's halfway house. She had her own room at Casa and worked as a clerical assistant in the hospital. She participated in group therapy with other disabled adolescents three times per week, plus individual counseling twice per week.

Counseling was focused on identifying and defusing her hyperarousal triggers. People who experience psychogenic non-epileptic seizures have triggers such as certain sights or sounds or people that greatly increase their anxiety, pushing them over the edge into a seizure. The seizure is a type of forced time-out, removing them from interacting with the trigger. Because it is often effective, it is a reinforced behavior; the person is unconsciously learning how to handle these triggers. Of course, the learned behavior is terribly maladaptive, so the triggers need to be defused through systematic desensitization like I used with Charlie in chapter 4, and other counseling strategies.

We also set up a contingency management (CM) program for Judy that helped her learn to avoid and manage her triggers so that her seizures decreased in frequency and eventually ceased entirely. This is especially helpful for people who are passive, which characterized Judy's personality. Her CM program rewarded her for making choices, such as asserting her right to proper interpersonal boundaries. Decorating her room at Casa was a self-directed experience in which she learned to assert her desires appropriately. Along with the other patients in her therapy group she studied *Your Perfect Right*, an excellent book now in its ninth edition for people learning how to stand up for themselves.

In retrospect, there were several important reasons for Judy's success, leading to our current aggregation of evidence for the efficacy of treating psychogenic non-epileptic seizures, such as:

1. Cognitive behavior therapy to reconfigure stress triggers[248]
2. Bedtime prayers of gratitude[136]
3. Encouraging secure love relationships[71]
4. Improving nutrition [249-251] and physical fitness[252]
5. Heart rhythm biofeedback training[253-255]
6. Personal prayer relaxation training[137-139, 256]
7. Homework to participate in moral and prosocial activities[120, 257, 258]
8. Increasing exposure to and participation in laughter[259, 260]

CBT helps restore brain integration, moving us toward the original design of our brains. Brain-based Christian counseling uses CBT in the context of a relationship with God because beginning our vertical integration with God provides the moral compass we need to optimally fit within God's reality.

I decided to include Judy's story because the underlying theme of her recovery and the context for all these techniques is God's love. These interventions are all effective in a secular treatment setting but seem to be optimized if we're able to settle into the certain and non-contingent love of God. In the next chapter, we will explore this further as we talk about a new type of love made available through Jesus.

Chapter Takeaways

1. Your brain and heart are vertically integrated.
2. The vagal nervous system helps the heart and brain communicate.
3. Thoughts originating in your brain are communicated by the vagus nerve to your heart.
4. Your vagus nerve communicates the responses of your heart to your brain.
5. Vagus nerve tone is crucial to healthy heart-brain balance.
6. Uncertainty that creates fear can be countered by the certainty of God's love.
7. Inviting God into our lives optimizes the benefits of heart-brain-balance therapies.

Discussion Questions

1. How well do your heart and brain communicate? How easily do you laugh or cry?
2. What are some examples of vagal nerve tone you would like to improve?
3. Do your relationships affect your vagus nerve tone positively or negatively?
4. What can you do to improve your vagal nerve tone?

CHAPTER 7

A Faithful Brain Is Loving

> Love is patient, love is kind. Love does not envy, it does not boast, it is not proud. Love does not dishonor others, it is not self-seeking, it is not easily angered; it keeps no record of wrongs. Love does not delight in evil but rejoices with the truth. Love always protects, always trusts, always hopes, always perseveres. Love never fails.
> —*1 Corinthians 13:4–8*

Brain Basics

1. Your brain-restorative capacities are optimally developed by the new covenant love of Jesus.
2. "Love the Lord your God with all your heart and soul and mind ... love your neighbor as yourself" is the best guidance for brain health.
3. Through improved brain health, love promotes your emotional health.
4. Through improved emotional health, love promotes your physical health.

"You're not being fair!"

Almost every couple who comes to me for marriage counseling eventually accuses each other of this, sometimes so often that it's the theme song of their marriage. Bob and Alice walk in the door shouting it and other angry words at each other and sit down with excess gravity in the armchairs at either end of my coffee table. Harrumph!

"What seems to be the problem?" I politely ask without needing to know.

"We agreed that our marriage would be fifty-fifty, but Bob's not holding up his end of the bargain! We decided I'd put my career on hold and stay home to raise the kids. It's more like ninety-ten, with me on the losing end. I'm sick and tired of it, and I won't put up with it any longer! I do the laundry, cooking, shopping, dishes, housecleaning, running the kids to school and soccer and taking care of them when they're sick, and he just goes to work and comes home and sits down with a beer and watches Sports Center until I've got dinner ready!

"If I ask him a question, he barely acknowledges me, and heaven forbid if I were to ask him to stop the kids from fighting in the middle of a football game! He'll explode at us all, and that just make things worse! I'm sick and tired of it, and I'm not going to take it anymore!"

Whenever I read Alice's diatribe to an audience of married couples in a marriage workshop, most of the women nod their heads knowingly, and most of the men shake their heads knowingly. Most of the women are willing to endorse Alice's experience, if not exactly their own pretty close to it. But I can't get many men to stick up for Bob. Why's that?

It's because everybody in the room believes Alice is right.

But if Alice is right, why do American men die on average five to six years younger than women, with stress a major culprit? Is it Bob's beer while watching Sports Center?

No, of course it's not the beer or Sports Center. Both Bob and Alice are under attack by modern culture, and a very effective solution to their distress is the new covenant love of Jesus.

What Is "New Covenant Love"?

The description of love in the letter from the apostle Paul to the Corinthians is recited at many weddings to encourage the newlyweds to develop a secure marriage with Jesus at its center. Paul presented the many facets of this love as a new standard. I like to describe this as *new covenant love*, indicating the new relationship with God that was brought to humanity by Jesus. We can learn to love unconditionally with complete trust and willing sacrifice by Jesus' example.

When I work with couples contemplating marriage, I encourage them to set new covenant love as their target, which is broader and deeper than any human love.[261]

New covenant love is the self-sacrificial love Jesus offers, undoing our human-limited ability to love. It is "all-powerful, untameable," like a hurricane bending a tree "beneath the weight of his wind and mercy."[7] New covenant love shreds our bark and splits us to our human core while bathing us in a safe and confident eternity.

New covenant love promotes secure relationships because it's self-sacrificial. Rather than fifty-fifty, new covenant love is one hundred–one hundred. The ultimate model for this was Jesus, whose servant heart and ultimate sacrifice gives

---

[7] Thanks to John Mark McMillan and Chris Tomlin for these powerful word images.

him the authority to instruct us on love. Scie[...]
of love such as this as coming out of "secure [...]
relationships.[63, 262-265] Neuroscience now confir[...]
is the path to optimal brain health and devel[...]
and Alice don't appreciate that their fifty-fifty attempt at fairness in marriage is doomed to mediocrity, setting them up to survive their marriage rather than have it flourish. This is because fifty-fifty marriages don't encourage the growth in the partners as do new covenant marriages.

The patterns of brain circuits that develop as we learn to love depend on the security of the love we experience.[266-269] We need secure love relationships in which we learn how to love by experiencing love[63, 263, 270-272] first with our parents and then with others. The experience of secure love develops brain circuits that are dedicated to love.[69, 268, 269] Through its moderating effect on stress, loving relationships protect neuroplasticity and neurogenesis,[32, 273] especially during early life.[274, 275] It now appears certain that a mother's love encourages neural epigenesis in fetuses and infants with lifelong health effects.[78, 276-278]

Although love can be wonderful, it's sometimes difficult and often risky. The most painful emotional experiences occur when love is lost. When we lose love, the emotional pain involves many of the same brain circuits as those activated by physical pain.[279-281] Because of this, we often limit our love to what we can tolerate, fearing the potential pain of lost love.

In contrast, as we experience the security of new covenant love in a relationship with God, using Jesus as our model, we expand our ability to trust and thereby our potential for human love. Flowing from his love, we further develop our capacity for love. New covenant lovers explore each other as if treasure were always about to be revealed. The other's imperfections beauty marks and cherished quirks. New covenant lovers assume potential in the other and yearn for opportunities to encourage growth. Both meanings of *appreciate* are active in new covenant love relationships. Marriages that are fifty-fifty experience only one type of appreciation, and then only on special occasions. In new covenant marriages, both types of appreciation are daily fare. Fairness and keeping score are irrelevant in new covenant marriages.

Is Marriage Necessary?

Not if it is merely a contract marriage, in which fifty-fifty fairness is more important than self-sacrifice. I often use Pastor Gary Chapman's popular press book, *Covenant Marriage* to help couples appreciate the difference between covenant and contract marriage. From a brain health and fitness perspective, a new covenant marriage is the crucible in which the trust demanded in a committed marriage is forged. A new covenant marriage resolves our brain's negativity bias that contaminates our ability to trust. It does this by helping us to practice risk, the necessary antidote to negativity bias. Hiding from risk increases our negativity bias, experienced as increasing anxiety and self-protective behavior. This is the trap into which people fall when they encounter PTSD triggers, which can be treated if the person is willing to practice risk by gradually re-experiencing the trigger so that the memory of the trauma is separated from its powerful emotional reaction. The best place to practice risk is within a new covenant marriage in which each person has the other's back, no questions asked.

We can more easily maintain distance from our lover if we're not married or if it's only a contract marriage. Without a new covenant marriage we can avoid the anxiety of trust and not practice risk. In contrast, if we take the marriage commitment seriously and go all-in and use Jesus as our model for character development, we have no choice but to grow beyond ourselves, trust our beloved, and practice risk. Practicing risk within a new covenant love relationship leads to an upward spiral in which anxiety is diminished and self-confidence is restored. Practicing risk this way gradually develops the ability to trust as it modifies the neural circuits devoted to emotional pain and improves our resilience.

New covenant marriage is especially important for our children. Sacrificial love in marriage helps parents develop the capacity for sacrificial love of their children. Children settle into secure attachment when they experience their parents' sacrificial love. Although becoming a parent certainly helps develop our sacrificial capacity, it's much better to learn ahead of time with our spouse.

New covenant love is especially important if we've been poorly-parented or if our parents were poorly-parented. Insecure relationships are enduring[282] and can be passed from generation to generation.[283] The biblical narrative in Exodus 20:5-6 describing the sins of the parents passed down through three or four generations is created as poor parenting uses neural epigenesis (chapter 2) to created unhealthy neural networks in the child's brain. This need not continue if we give Jesus' love a chance to develop secure relationships with our spouse and then with our children. Repairing parents' insecure attachments is one of the strongest arguments for a new covenant marriage as the context for emotionally healthy child development.

Becoming new covenant lovers in marriage isn't just theoretical for me. I was married and divorced three times before I was thirty. I began to explore the character of Jesus after I met Mary. Although we began with a contract marriage because I didn't know any better, Mary and I now share a new covenant marriage. During our courtship and early marriage, she patiently encouraged me to explore the teachings of Jesus. I was intrigued but skeptical. I tried to keep an open mind and noticed that we kept circling back to grace, God's unwavering and inexhaustible gift of love personified by Jesus. Gradually, my neuroplasticity was harnessed by his grace.

I now love Mary and my family more completely than I ever could have imagined. I had loved before, but I had not allowed myself to be loved by God personified in Jesus. My belief in God when I was a child and adolescent didn't extend to a love relationship with Jesus. After our marriage, I gradually fell in love with God's Son. My new covenant relationship with Jesus helped me to glimpse what was possible, to be available for love beyond the limits I had mistakenly accepted. My love relationship with Jesus expanded my capacity for loving others because my human love relationships use many of the same neural networks. [284-286] In turn, Mary guided me as we developed the loving brain-heart circuits in our children that they took into adolescence and adulthood.[287]

Can I Learn New Covenant Love outside Marriage?

New covenant love is difficult to learn within marriage let alone outside the commitment marriage requires. It takes more time and transparency than we usually allow and much more trust than is normally available outside of marriage, but it's not impossible.

I have a friend who is a single father with two adult daughters with whom he shares new covenant love relationships. Though they live separate lives, they intentionally set aside one evening a week to have dinner or go to a movie. Every summer, they take a vacation together, just the three of them. Along with this unusual time commitment, they maintain healthy transparency and discuss some of the intimate details of their lives, including my friend's commitment to celibacy until he remarries.

Transparency is the hallmark of new covenant love relationships. Asking each partner to extend an "umbrella of grace" to the other, I encourage couples to experiment with increasing their transparency so they can develop new covenant love relationships. Grace is necessary because becoming more transparent is often risky. The reason not to be transparent is often a concern about embarrassment or shame. Divulging embarrassing thoughts, attitudes, and experiences is risky. If this can be done in the context of grace, the person practicing transparency will be more likely to undertake what Alcoholics Anonymous calls "a searching and fearless moral inventory" and consider sharing it with their loved ones. This must be done thoughtfully and carefully so more harm is not done because each of us has been less than perfect.

I actively work on new covenant love relationships with my adult children by appropriately sharing with them some of the intimate details of my current and past life. I don't demand they share at that level with me, but that tends to happen. Though we're thousands of miles distant, we communicate regularly and support each other in times of crisis. We all have somewhat different values, but we're careful to be respectful. I also offer new covenant love relationships to my children's spouses and to my grandchildren. These are more difficult to develop and maintain, but making the ongoing effort is worth it.

I have a few friends with whom I am in committed relationships, but these are very few compared to all the friendships I share. I know that we are in committed relationships because we hold no secrets; these men are my transparency partners. With these few people, I can ask any question and expect an honest answer, and I hold myself to that standard. Any of them could use my personal passwords without any concern from me that my private life would be mishandled. From these people I have transparency like my transparency with my wife. The only areas that are private involve my professional client files.

I try to begin a transparency partner relationship with people other than my wife when I share my Goaling Life Plan, as Carol did in chapter 3. Depending on their response, we may begin to develop a new covenant love relationship. Reciprocal trust and respect and grace are sometimes signaled when a Life Plan is shared, which is a wonderful affirmation that the other person is worthy of your trust. This may be the start of a committed relationship that goes beyond the "friends" we know through social media.

How would it be for all parents to have frank, open, and caring discussions with their adolescent and young adult children about sexuality? How would it be to have several people in your life who are able to access your personal files, smart phone, or laptop history? It's not that they would do it; it's more about being so transparent with your life that this wouldn't matter. New covenant love outside marriage takes a lot of work and some risk, but it's worth pursuing.

What's the Neuroscience of Love?

Christian neuroscientists agree that our brains develop and function optimally when we follow Jesus' guidance in Matthew 22:37–39: "Love the Lord your God with all your heart and soul and mind, and love your neighbor as yourself."

We often forget that Jesus was brilliant.[288] Just as important, we allow others to bypass this aspect of his being. His genius is evident in stories of his debates with the religious zealots and scholars of the day,[87] in the depth of his parables, and in his sermons.[289] Jesus' emphasis on loving relationships and our brain's need for loving relationships is not just a coincidence; our brains develop and function optimally when immersed in secure love relationships.[286, 287, 290-292] Many powerful brain mechanisms use love as their fuel and secure love relationships as their vehicle. From the womb to the deathbed, brain renewal processes are promoted and protected by love.

By focusing on God's love, Jesus helped most of his disciples to feel, think, and behave in ways that we now know were faithful to the design of their brains. To the degree that each disciple was able to surrender, the relationship allowed Jesus to change his brain. With his nurturing love, all but one of the disciples developed values, beliefs, and goals that transformed their lives. And it wasn't just Jesus' loving and patient treatment of his disciples that was noteworthy. The respectful and inclusive way that Jesus related to women in first-century Palestine was considered revolutionary and was transformative for each of them. Anyone feeling trapped in a less-than-optimal life should be encouraged by the transformative potential of a relationship with Jesus.

Remember that Jesus didn't just lecture; he showed us how to live. Jesus was an example to his disciples and can be ours. As Dallas Willard wrote, "Follow Jesus, and if you can find a better way than him, he would be the first one to tell you to take it."[293] By following his example, each of us has the opportunity to participate with God's processes for healthy brain development, perhaps beginning with the effects of oxytocin on cortisol.

What Are Oxytocin and Cortisol?

In the brain, the experience of love is closely related to *oxytocin*. Oxytocin is a *neuropeptide* produced in the *hypothalamus* and stored in the posterior *pituitary* gland that's released when we give or receive love. Oxytocin is one of 90 neuropeptides that help neurons communicate, often in concert with another class of proteins called neurotransmitters. The production and release of oxytocin is stimulated by loving intimate and social interaction. [71, 294, 295] You were introduced to oxytocin at birth when:

> **Oxytocin**
> A brain chemical that promotes strong relationships and bonding.

1. Oxytocin triggered your mother's birth contractions. [296]
2. Your mother first held you and oxytocin flooded both bodies, bonding you to each other.[297]
3. Your suckling at her breast produced more oxytocin in her brain, deepening the bond.[298]

The effect of oxytocin on your mother during your early infancy broadened her experience of love beyond what she had experienced as a wife.[71] And throughout your life, loving relationships have produced oxytocin in your body as well.

In adulthood, oxytocin helps balance other brain
One of the most important involves modulating t
and potentially detrimental effects of *cortisol* [299]
health and development directly and by calming anxiety.[302]

Cortisol is circulating in your body at all times to help you maintain adequate metabolism as you respond to challenges. Cortisol helps break down fats, proteins, and carbohydrates into glucose to be used for energy.

Cortisol is normally highest in the morning as your brain gets you ready for the challenges of the day after fasting for several hours while you slept.[303] If you have

> **Cortisol**
>
> A chemical that helps break down fats, proteins, and carbohydrates to maintain metabolism.

a nice, calm day with no serious challenges, cortisol gradually ebbs to its lowest level just before you drop off to sleep at night.[304]

Cortisol increases rapidly in response to stressful challenges as part of the "fight or flight" response[305] triggered by the amygdala. Along with the release of fast-acting chemicals such as *epinephrine* (adrenaline) and *norepinephrine* (noradrenaline), cortisol helps support your ongoing response to a challenge.

Cortisol is longer lasting than epinephrine and norepinephrine and hangs around at its stress-elevated levels longer than the other chemicals. Even after you're no longer challenged and the epinephrine has stopped flowing, cortisol remains elevated in your bloodstream. Instead of gradually dropping off over the course of the day, every time you're challenged, cortisol spikes. Because modern lives are full of challenges, cortisol may be triggered several times a day and sometimes all day for several days. If you're being challenged continuously, cortisol remains abnormally high all day long.[306]

Elevated cortisol at bedtime interferes with brain-restorative sleep, the first step in the onset of many illnesses.[304] Prolonged cortisol elevation may also interfere with neurogenesis, stunt growth, and cause the death of new neurons in the hippocampus.[41, 129, 307] New neurons need relationships, so attempts to link up with other neurons are very important. High levels of cortisol may stunt these linkages. If a neuron can't develop sufficient relationships with other neurons, it will die.

How Does Love Restore My Brain?

Love protects and restores your brain in many ways, starting with oxytocin. Neuroscience has confirmed that oxytocin:

1. Improves a child's ability to handle stress[294]
2. Improves the ability to recover from illness[308]
3. Hastens the healing of wounds[66, 309]
4. Improves the ability to handle pain[310]
5. Encourages novelty seeking and creativity[311]
6. Minimizes your response to fearful images[312, 313]
7. Improves social comfort and heart rate variability[314]
8. Protects against atherosclerosis[315]
9. Promotes secure attachment relationships[70, 290, 296, 316-318]
10. Helps with the social behavioral deficits of people with obsessive-compulsive disorder, depression, social anxiety disorder, borderline personality disorder, schizophrenia, and autism-spectrum disorders[71, 117, 118, 314, 319-321]

Oxytocin improves connections between the brain regions associated with discernment and the amygdala, where your "fight or flight" response originates. The improved connectivity helps down-regulate or calm the amygdala.[302, 305, 313, 322]

You can decrease unnecessarily elevated cortisol by increasing oxytocin. Synthetic oxytocin administered as a nasal spray decreases the cortisol response to physical stress and social rejection.[299, 300] Oxytocin is available as a prescription medication to help women lactate and induce labor. Oxytocin nasal spray is being considered as a treatment for the social isolation found in autism-spectrum disorders.

The natural approach to increase oxytocin occurs through secure love relationships with a spouse, children, parents, siblings, friends, and pets. Secure love relationships produce oxytocin in both halves of the brain.[70, 295] Oxytocin love can also involve animals, as Clowny did with Peter and Judy and many other children at Rancho.[323] In my work with U.S. service members back from combat who experience post-traumatic stress disorder (PTSD) and/or traumatic brain injury, I strongly recommend their involvement with a service dog. The calming influence of the love relationship has deep psychophysical roots and improves mood, sleep, and cognitive function.

Beyond the effect of oxytocin that comes from love relationships, love benefits the brain in many other ways. Love and trust foster healthy brain development for emotional processing and self-regulation.[286, 287, 292, 324] These affect the actual structure of the brain and can be measured in the frontal cortex,[292, 324, 325] the right hemisphere,[292, 324] and the corpus callosum[326] of children.

If we want to evaluate brain restoration, we must make comparisons of the same brain many years apart. Because neuroscience is a new field of study, these longitudinal studies are brief and rare, so we don't yet know the specific restorative effects of love on the brain. But we do know that "scars" on the emotional centers of the brain caused by childhood neglect and abuse are years later found in the adult brain. [327] While there's some early evidence that brain changes due to neglect can be reversed by immersion in love relationships and nurturing environments,[328] we're not sure how this works. But supplementing the limited scientific findings we have thus far are powerful anecdotal reports of love restoring brain health and function after severe abuse, such as the *Child of Rage* HBO documentary.[329]

Until we have many more longitudinal studies that allow us to study the effects of love on brain health over time, we will need to make the assumption that brain health is reflected by general health. The best current examples of how love affects health come from studies of the effects of marriage on health and the effects of faith and religious practices on health.

How Does Marriage Affect My Health?

The effects of marriage on health are numerous. It's not marriage itself but the quality of the marriage that makes a difference. A review of 126 studies of marital quality and health that involved more than 70,000 participants found in study after study that better marital quality was consistently related to better physical health. Cardiovascular disease, lower pain-related disability, physical mobility, dental health, kidney disease, re-hospitalization after heart attacks, days in the hospital after surgery, and wound healing[330] were better for those in healthy marriages.

When psychological health is considered, good marital quality seems to protect you from depression. Marital quality was a stronger predictor of physical health than was cigarette smoking or the use of alcohol or the effect of exercise on health; the better your marriage, the better your health. Following these trends, better marital quality also was related to lower risk of death.[331, 332]

The health effects of marriage are likely due to several biologic mediators.[333] For example, high levels of supportive behavior within the marriage are related to lower stress hormone levels.[334] When newlyweds in a solid marriage encounter trouble, they handle the trouble better and their bodies produce lower levels of cortisol.[335]

Outside stressors, such as those from work, are handled better by each person in a solid marriage, especially the wife.[336] Wives' cortisol levels rise and fall with their own work stress and with their husbands' work stress, while husbands' cortisol levels seem to be tied only to their work stress.[337] Most importantly, women who talked with their husbands about their own problems at work had lower levels of work-related cortisol compared with women who didn't share their concerns. This is a hint about what is happening with Bob and Alice. Alice's sharing of her frustration is a therapeutic outlet for her that Bob doesn't use.

Aside from stress from the workplace, in a high-quality marriage, each person's daily cortisol pattern tends to be synchronized with the other's cortisol level, on awakening and throughout the day, and is elevated when either reports loneliness.[338, 339] Married couples' fluctuations in negative mood and cortisol levels are linked; when one is down, the other tends to be down.[340] But marital satisfaction seems to buffer each person from their spouse's negative mood; a good marriage minimizes the effect of one person's bad mood on the other. So in a good marriage, Alice can vent therapeutically while Bob listens with respect and attention and doesn't try to fix her situation. When Alice is done venting, she asks, "Honey, tell me about your day," pours a glass of wine, and sits down to listen to her man, whose life would otherwise be shortened by forty-five minutes by the stress of that day.

Forty-five minutes? Do the math for the life expectancy of a middle-aged married American male and you'll understand why Alice needs to listen and Bob needs to talk. Wouldn't it be nice if they could both die within hours of each other in old age, holding hands and still feeling the heartbeat of love? Alice doesn't want to spend her last five years without Bob, so she listens and encourages Bob to talk. If they can develop the habit of disclosing their fears, joys, trials, and triumphs to each other, they're well on the way to developing a new covenant marriage.

Are There Many New Covenant Marriages?

Yes, this is a wonderful area of growth in modern society! Pastor Andy Sharpe and his wife Lisa, who is one of my counseling practice partners, offer a six-week marriage workshop each year that is attended by hundreds of couples. Using Gary Chapman's book, *Covenant Marriage* and material from Archibald Hart and Sharon May, Peter Scazzero, Willard Harley, and Emerson Eggerichs, they bring to awareness the ever-present opportunity for new covenant marriage. The workshop series is always over-subscribed; people are hungry for what Andy and Lisa have to offer.

This morning, I had the opportunity to hear about the burgeoning new covenant marriage of one of my graduate students. Mandy is a woman in her early thirties who had a long history of depression for which she had been successfully treated with counseling and antidepressant medication. After her marriage six years ago, she consulted with her psychiatrist and husband and began to gradually back off her medication. Over the past thirty months, Mandy has navigated graduate school and new motherhood without the need of medication.

> It really is true! Jerry's touch and looks and words help me feel alive and put my problems in perspective. I think I do the same for him. When I wake up worried, I can just reach over and touch him and I feel myself relax. It was very different, being much more open and honest with him than I had been with anyone, even my parents and sister. But we've both grown together in transparency and love.

Mandy's experience is no longer rare. My colleagues and I routinely counsel couples before marriage and early in their marriages to consider making a commitment to go beyond a contract marriage. For most couples, this seems to be a new idea. They find it intriguing and often ask me to explain the difference between contract and covenant marriages, which they easily grasp. I often hear that they know at least one other couple who seems to be in a new covenant marriage, and I ask what about that couple they find attractive. Typically, I hear that it's something about each person being more relaxed, comfortable, and confident. I point out that these are the opportunities for growth each person has in a covenant marriage based on the model of sacrificial love God offered to us in Jesus.

I'm seeing increased desire to develop new covenant marriages in my practice, especially as Baby Boomers age. I find that those who can make a commitment to the combination of transparency and grace most easily transition from contract marriages to covenant marriages. The transition is difficult, but many couples successfully make it. Couples who are marrying after divorce or widowhood eagerly embrace the opportunity to develop a new covenant marriage. I provide counseling and recommend appropriate reading (see next section). I may also recommend a mentor couple with whom they can meet for encouragement and guidance. I talk about the "umbrella of grace" we need to offer that is so necessary to encourage transparency and help develop trust. The opportunity to experience profound love for the rest of their lives within the context of a new covenant marriage is very attractive!

How Does Loving God Promote My Health?

Jesus instructed us to begin with, "Love the Lord your God" because God's love is the best starting point for all our love relationships. At least that's how it has been for me and thousands of my clients. As I look at my secular-psychologist-to-Christian-psychologist transition more than twenty-five years ago, the most important difference in me is the attitude I bring to my work. I am more sensitive to the beliefs of my clients[341] and more often encourage my clients to explore God's love. I recommend pertinent stories in the *Celebrate Recovery Bible*.[1] I loan accessible books I have read by authors such as David Gregory,[342] Brennan Manning,[343] Og Mandino,[344] Phillip Yancey,[132] and Rick Warren.[261] For people who appreciate more-challenging reading, my favorite recommendation is C. S. Lewis's *Mere Christianity*.[345]

In recent years, I have recommended William Young's *The Shack*[346] to my clients who are exploring Christianity. The story revolves around the abduction from a family camping trip and the later murder of six-year-old Missy, the youngest daughter of Mack, who falls into "the Great Sadness" that emotionally paralyzes him. As the story unfolds, Mack meets God, Jesus, and the Holy Spirit at a shack in the woods near where Missy was killed, and he explores his loss. As the Great Sadness begins to lift, Mack says,

"There is one thing still bothering me about Missy."

> Jesus walked over and sat next to him on the log. Mack leaned over and put his elbows on his knees, staring past his hands and down at the pebbles near his feet. Finally, he said, "I keep thinking about her, alone in that truck, so terrified …"

> Jesus reached over and put his hand on Mack's shoulder and squeezed. Gently, he spoke, "Mack, she was never alone. I never left her; we never left her not for one instant. I could no more abandon her or you than I could abandon myself."

> "Did she know you were there?"

> "Yes, Mack, she did. Not at first—the fear was overwhelming and she was in shock. It took hours to get up here from the campsite. But as Sarayu (Holy Spirit) wrapped herself around her, Missy settled down. The long ride actually gave us a chance to talk."

Mack was trying to take all of this in. He could no longer speak.

"She may have been only six years old, but Missy and I are friends. We talk. She had no idea what was going to happen. She actually worried more about you and the other kids, knowing that you couldn't find her. She prayed for you, for your peace."

Mack wept, fresh tears rolling down his cheeks. This time, he didn't mind. Jesus gently pulled him into his arms and held him.

"Mack, I don't think you want to know all the details. I'm sure they won't help you. But I can tell you that there was not a moment that we were not with her. She knew my peace and you would have been proud of her. She was so brave!" ([346] page 173)

Many of us have experienced the love of God during difficult times. As we read about Missy and Mack, Jesus followers know the truth of God's love, and we feel sad but hopeful. Available when our logical, linear, left brain integrates with our pattern-seeking right brain, the love of God brings heartfelt peace that rings true and engages us fully. Our scars begin to heal. The courage and confidence necessary to live life to the full, as an adventure in a broken world, take root and begin to grow. As neuroscience explores the brain basis and intertwined heart of these feelings, we will always trust the truth of our experience.

God's love extends beyond our intimate love relationship and into the larger community, usually through participation in church and religious activities.[168, 169, 261]

While early studies of the health effects of spirituality, religious activities, and church participation were discouraging,[347, 348] several recent studies[349-353] strongly support the idea that faith and some religious practices buffer stress and promote longer, healthier lives. Simply put, most modern scientific studies demonstrate that people who actively participate in faith and religious activities live longer than those who don't.[354, 355] The second edition of the *Handbook of Religion and Health*[356] considered more than 2,800 studies that examine the relationships between religion/spirituality and health. More than two-thirds of the studies report a significant positive effect and less than 15 percent report a negative relationship between health and religious practices.

A subsequent study that was focused on mental health found that religious faith was positively related to most but not all mental disorders.[357] For example, studies focused on dementia, suicide, and stress-related disorders showed uniformly positive effects of religious practices, while studies that considered bipolar disorder were mixed or negative.

The breadth and complexity of the relationships among religious practices and health is bringing about a growing awareness that scientists and the faith community must work together. As the authors of the *Handbook* report put it,

> The twin healing traditions of religion and medicine have slowly split apart over the past 500 years. Within the last decade, however, there are signs that the gap between these two traditions may be closing. Research has shown that medical patients have religious

iritual needs intimately related to their
 l health that can influence their medical
 ιs and can often be important for coping
 ιess.

Psychoneuroimmunology and psychosomatic medicine are shedding light on the physiological mechanisms by which psychological, social, and behavioral factors can affect physical health. These mechanisms provide us with rational and highly plausible explanations for how and why religion may impact physical as well as mental health-quite apart from supernatural influences that are beyond scientific investigation.([356] page 604)

The health effects of faith and spirituality continue to be revealed in the scientific literature on a frequent basis. This is an important focus of research at the Faithful Brain Foundation, where we are especially interested in post-traumatic growth (PTG). As with Peter in chapter 1, a very traumatic experience can bring about a change in life that creates a new and healthier trajectory. PTG is a relatively new area of scientific research[358, 359] with broad implications for society and medicine and thereby faith and religious institutions. My work with persons who have severe traumatic disabilities suggests that PTG extends broadly to all serious illnesses and injuries.

In my non-hospital practice with people who have experienced severe emotional trauma without physical disability, many of the same dynamics seem to be involved. As my friend Russ Kirkland assures me, "God won't waste anything!" Trauma, no matter how severe, is integrated by God into the created reality in which we were all designed to prosper.

Chapter Takeaways

1. "Love the Lord your God with all your heart and soul and mind ... love your neighbor as yourself" is fully compatible with neuroscience, supporting the growth and health of your brain.
2. You learn to love more fully by experiencing God's love.
3. You are called to love relationships modeled after your relationship with Jesus.
4. Love is your first experience in life, fundamentally bonding us to each other at birth.
5. Love helps to restore the balance among neurochemicals such as oxytocin and cortisol.
6. Love promotes your brain health and physical health and emotional health.

Discussion Questions

1. Do you experience new covenant love?
2. What does offering new covenant love to your spouse, family, or friends do for your quality of life.
3. What does offering new covenant love to your spouse, family, or friends do for the recipient?
4. What can you do to increase oxytocin in your brain and the brains of those you love?

CHAPTER 8

A Faithful Brain Is Grace-Blessed

For the law was given through Moses; grace and truth came through Jesus Christ
—*John 1:17*

Brain Basics

1. Embarrassment, shame, and disgust are some of the corrective emotions triggered by guilt.
2. Corrective emotions arise when you're guilty of behaviors counter to your values.
3. Corrective emotions are processed in the brain's default mode network (DMN).
4. The DMN is the center of your conscience and personal morality.
5. As you experience God's grace, corrective emotions guide your choices.
6. As you choose to fit within God's created reality, quality-of-life improves.

What Is Grace?

A key moment in my journey back to God occurred when a wise man asked me if I understood why grace comes before truth in this verse from the gospel of John. Pastor Richard Burdine posed this question to his congregation at the Community United Methodist Church in Huntington Beach, California, at the start of my first church service after more than ten years as a failed anti-theist. Standing next to Mary, the woman God had sent to help rescue me from my pride and depravity, it seemed a simple question, but I didn't have an answer.

> **Grace**
>
> God's unwavering and inexhaustible love that pursues us through our rebellion, calling us back and into relationship.

Pastor Dick paused to let us consider the question before gripping the sides of his lectern and standing on his tiptoes and yelling at me, "Because without grace you can't stand the truth!" Grace is God's unwavering and inexhaustible gift of love beyond what words can describe.

I'm glad Dick yelled at me because I needed to hear him clearly. Actually, he had yelled at about 300 people in a packed sanctuary on that Sunday morning more than thirty years ago. But he seemed to look right at me, a young man he had not yet met, because somehow he knew I needed to hear him clearly.

I not only needed to hear Pastor Dick *clearly*, I needed to hear him *badly*. I was deeply troubled. I had spent the prior ten years pursuing the American dream without God. Outwardly, I appeared to be successful, but I was depressed and exhausted and had just given up the idea of suicide. I badly needed to hear about grace, God's unwavering and inexhaustible love beyond what words can describe. I hadn't yet discovered that grace was an unearned gift flowing from God that allows us to face the truth about our inherent inadequacy.

I had been blinded by my pride as I tried to live without God. Unceasing anxiety and my emotional and spiritual emptiness led to depression. It seemed to me that surrendering my culturally successful standard of living was necessary but impossible. I felt trapped in my own expensive and impressive mess and couldn't see my way out. It was a very dark and powerful trap because my pride had blinded me to my need for God. I thought I needed to save myself. I didn't yet understand that God had sent Jesus to save even people like me.

I now understand that our brain was designed for redemption and rehabilitation. This occurs in part through the *corrective emotions* that occur when we're involved in something that doesn't square with our values. I introduced you to corrective emotions in chapter 3, when you heard about Carol and how she was struggling with another person's poor choices.

> **Corrective Emotions**
> Automatic physiologic responses triggered by our brain in reaction to a choice that is at odds with our values.

When our choices aren't aligned with our values, emotions such as regret and guilt are triggered, followed by embarrassment, shame, and self-disgust in an increasingly painful cycle. If we know we're guilty of our behaviors, we may acknowledge this pain as deserved, take responsibility, apologize, and try to make amends. But we often sidestep the guilt and shirk this responsibility. We may even blame others for our pain.

Sometimes, the pain of corrective emotions can be soul-suffocating because the truth about our choice ugly that we think it can't be faced. This is the lie that tries to justify suicide and this is the truth that is too painful for us to stand on our own. For me, trying to hide from this truth led to three failed marriages before I was 30. I had dodged the regret and guilt of my irresponsibility and avoided the embarrassment and shame of my behavior by becoming mindless in Southern California. The infected blisters of my self-disgust festered, temporarily salved by alcohol and other substances, and erupted in rare moments of painful clarity. The destructive effects of my unaddressed corrective emotions were unavoidable and I began to consider suicide. To face this ugly truth and become available to healing required God's grace, which I learned about when Mary insisted that our first "date" be at Pastor Dick's church.

Why Are Corrective Emotions Necessary?

Corrective emotions are very powerful and may cause us to change our behaviors or they may continue to be corrosive, it's our choice. My early training as a secular psychologist had led me to believe that these emotions were to be avoided or minimized. I now understand that this was a mistake that subverts the design of our brain and can set the stage for many problems.

Significant behavioral change often requires pain. If we're comfortable in our own skin, we don't feel the need to change. When a client sits on my couch and tells me a story that triggers uncomfortable corrective emotions, I am hopeful; I know we're on the verge of change. But change is so much easier if my client has been introduced to God's grace. This is especially true for anxiety and depression.

The scientific gold standard for treating anxiety and depression is cognitive behavior therapy (CBT). Its efficacy has been demonstrated in thousands of studies. Even the best medicines for anxiety and depression are insufficient unless they are paired with CBT. The key to CBT is that the client's pain is their motivation for change. The client is encouraged to try new thoughts and behaviors so the pain of their corrective emotions is relieved.

Before I became a Christian, I was well trained and moderately effective with CBT and its predecessors. But I now know I was helping my clients fight their anxiety and depression with one hand tied behind my back. I call what I now do Brain-Based Christian Counseling because integrating neuroscience with Christian faith is much more effective. The efficacy of faith combined with CBT is the focus of important new research at the Faithful Brain Institute and elsewhere.[360]

In his wonderful book *Tattoos on the Heart*, Father Gregory Boyle tells the story of his encounter with God's grace on a busy morning between masses and baptisms in East Los Angeles. He describes Carmen, a thirty-something heroin addict and sometime prostitute in her first visit to his office. The clock is ticking while he tries to get ready for a baptism ceremony. She tells him that she started using heroin right after high school and has been trying to stop from the moment she started.

> Then I watch as Carmen tilts her head back until it meets the wall. She stares at the ceiling and in an instant her eyes become these two ponds, water rising to meet their edges, swollen

> banks, spilling over. Then for the first time really, she looks at me and straightens.
>
> "I ... am ... a ... disgrace."
>
> Suddenly, her shame meets mine. When Carmen walked through that door, I had mistaken her for an interruption.([361] page 42)

Boyle described how God's ongoing grace in his life often provides these lessons. He explained that we mistakenly think that shame and sin happens to someone else. "My shame can't meet Carmen's unless I dispel that notion." This is why it's so important to me that pastors and counselors and psychologists and psychiatrists go through their own counseling. Unless we take the time and effort and hard work required to come to grips with the truth of our own brokenness we have only techniques to offer our clients. What people really want is our experience, strength, and hope. What people really need is our personal knowledge of God's healing grace.

How Does God's Grace Help Me?

I have found that without grace, we can't stand the truth, and believing we are a disgrace is so discouraging that it stops us from even trying. However, with grace we can explore the dark truth of our behaviors. Assured of God's love in spite of our brokenness, grace helps us see ourselves more clearly. We more readily accept that we're broken and we can become hopeful. We begin to understand God will never abandon us no matter what. We learn Jesus especially loved those who were embarrassed, ashamed, and disgusted with themselves. Their stories are examples of his healing grace.

In Brain-Based Christian Counseling, God's grace injects hope into cognitive behavior therapy and points the way to redemption. Grace is the optimal context for CBT because grace is the optimal context for the truth about how we can fit into God's created reality one day at a time, with our eyes on Jesus.

With Jesus, we have shelter from the storm of our corrective emotions under an umbrella of grace and are enabled to be honest with ourselves and others. As we experience the inexhaustible love of God, we can begin to admit our brokenness. Rather than committing valuable brain circuits to maintain the false protection of pride, grace allows corrective emotions to take their proper place, guiding us with emotional pain that we learn to trust is for our own good.

As I grew to trust God's love personified by Jesus, I more often took responsibility for my guilt-producing choices. Although excruciatingly difficult, I began to say "Thank you" for my embarrassment and shame and less often experienced regret and self-disgust. I gradually learned that the light of God's grace shines so bright that it eclipses the glare of my pride, an ongoing process that continues today. As I work on developing a faithful brain, the light of God's grace helps me see more clearly the inadequacies and fears that drive my pride. God's grace helps humility to be my choice more often. My prideful response to challenges and real or imagined slights becomes less prolonged and wasteful; I bow my head, thank God for the temporary pain and move on.

The Bible has many examples of grace helping corrective emotions bring about healthy change. My favorite example is Jesus' disciple Peter, who loved Jesus but denied knowing him when the chips were down. In the last hours before Jesus' crucifixion, Peter turned his back on Jesus three times and denied even knowing Him. How much embarrassment, shame, and disgust Peter must have felt! How miserable he must have been.

But in John 21, the Bible gives us the ultimate model of grace, as Jesus constructively used Peter's pain. On a cold early morning on a Palestinian beach, the resurrected Jesus started a campfire over which he cooked fish for breakfast. He invited Peter and his friends to join him. The smoke of the fire must have reminded Peter of the fire by which he warmed himself as he denied his friendship when Jesus was being attacked and mocked a few nights earlier. Though he deeply loved Jesus, he had denied knowing him three times during that long night.

Around the campfire, without mentioning Peter's betrayal, Jesus restored him by asking three times if Peter loved him. Each time, Peter answered "yes". Each yes was followed by a command from Jesus that became his marching orders to Peter to guide and nurture his church.

We now understand that Peter's emotional limbic system was fully engaged and gave powerful emotional salience to each of Jesus' questions and to each of Peter's responses. Not only would he never forget the words of Jesus, they would direct him for the rest of his life. We call this strong emotional salience "conviction"; Peter was convicted by the love of Jesus.

Smell is the only sense that is not conditioned by our thought processes. By setting the stage with the campfire, Jesus used the smell of smoke to go directly to Peter's limbic system and then down through the vagal nervous system to Peter's heart. In this way, Jesus bypassed the self-condemnation in Peter's cerebral cortex. Peter's disgust with his earlier refusal to acknowledge Jesus during that terrible night was completely short-circuited by Jesus' love. The neural patterns Peter had developed about Jesus in their previous three years together were then charged so powerfully by Jesus' grace that Peter became the rock upon which his church could be built. Peter's heart must have pounded mightily as he was restored by Jesus' grace and love!

What if I Don't Experience Corrective Emotions?

Some of us don't experience painful corrective emotions, and others are able to hide from our corrective emotions in fantasies that are made more possible by chemicals that impair clarity. We may have had horrible trauma in childhood that strongly dis-integrated our limbic system from our cerebral cortex. These may have been so powerful that we can make choices without emotional attachment. But even if we had such horrible childhood trauma, we must never forget that our brains are designed for redemption and rehabilitation; God never gives up. If we can accept the safety of God's love and grace and begin to explore our traumatic memories with an experienced counselor we'll find that the memories begin to become less painful. The brain actually reorganizes so that the links between our traumatic memories and the re-experiencing of emotional pain begin to weaken.

A wonderful example of the effect of approaching horrible childhood trauma within the context of God's love is driven home in *Child of Rage*, the HBO documentary of Beth, who was abused as a toddler and learned to be without corrective emotions in early childhood. I encourage you to find her story online; it's widely available.

I show the video of Beth's story to my introduction to the unlimited redemptive a[?] power of God's love. Because these are gra[?] Covenant Theological Seminary, they have a str[?] understanding of God's love and grace, but some have not y[?] appreciated its awesome power. They are profoundly affected by the intertwining of redemption and rehabilitation at the heart of Beth's story.

An important aspect of Beth's story is about the difference between offering grace and being nonjudgmental. As a secular counselor before I became a Christian, I tried to be nonjudgmental by carefully keeping my value judgments to myself and out of the counseling relationship. I adhered to the idea that each of us is responsible for creating our own reality and our own truth, necessitating the development of our own values.

Now, as a Christian counselor, with a client who is open to considering the values God has to offer, I initiate the discussion by describing my own inherent brokenness and sinful nature. We talk about the holy righteousness of God that cannot be modified to meet our circumstances or situation. But rather than despairing that we will always fall short, we discuss the offer Jesus makes available to bridge the gap and restore us to right-relationship with God. We discuss how grace flows from love that's beyond our ability to comprehend, requiring faith. Given my brain-based perspective, I describe to my clients how this makes possible ongoing changes in our brains that move us closer to how we were designed. As we move closer to our original design, our brains become more efficient, powerful, and healthy.

Where Does Grace Show Up in the Brain?

In the brain, we compare choices with our values in the default mode network (DMN), the seat of our social conscience. The DMN involves several brain regions that work together as we reflect on ourselves and our relationships with others.[362-365] The DMN begins to develop at birth and improves as we mature.[366] Distinct patterns in the DMN arise when we make moral judgments[367, 368] as well as with different types of psychopathology.[369] When the choice we make doesn't square with our moral code, the DMN triggers corrective emotions.[369]

When disease or injury disrupts these circuits so we can't experience corrective emotions, we exhibit inappropriate behavior.[370] Alternately, corrective emotions can spin up and out of control if we ruminate on a poor choice, which appears to set the stage for anxiety disorders and depression.[371-373]

In the brain, a phenomenon called error-related negativity (ERN) is a signal that arises in the anterior cingulate cortex less than one-tenth of a second after we make an error. The ERN signal is powerful in the brains of people suffering from anxiety disorders and is associated with decreased heart-rate variability and poor vagal nerve tone. Alcohol and other chemicals that diminish anxiety also diminish ERN.

Is there something we can use other than alcohol and anxiolytic medications such as Xanax to decrease error-related negativity? In a fascinating series of research studies,[374] the degree to which a person believed in God reduced error-related negativity. In the science-speak summary of this amazing research, "Religious primes lower the ERN." These scientists found that prayer and meditating on Scripture helps to lessen our negativity, which is measureable in the brain!

Grace allows the pain of our brokenness and its ugly and uncomfortable truth to be tempered by love in our DMN.

Grace helps us moderate pride and allows the emotions of embarrassment and shame to correct us without destroying us. Oxytocin and serotonin seem to be key agents in this process. This helps God harness our neuroplasticity long enough for us to consider values based on biblical truths. That's how it was with me. I needed God's grace to face my ugly truth and to begin to learn I was loved in spite of my brokenness.

Facing our ugly truth requires courage. In her wonderful book *The Gifts of Imperfection*,[375] scientist Brené Brown described this as "wholehearted living." From her personal and professional experience, "holding our story and loving ourselves through that process is the bravest thing that we will ever do."

Our brain, when it's grace-immersed in a trusting relationship with Jesus provides the final common pathway to the full potential of life. As our brain responds to grace, God uses its restorative capacities to guide our growth through cycles of increasingly honest moral inventories as we make amends, seek forgiveness, and drop resentment of others. As Brown wrote, "Cultivating a wholehearted life is not like trying to reach a destination. It's like walking toward a star in the sky. We never really arrive, but we certainly know that we are heading in the right direction."[375] We begin to realize that a power greater than ourselves can restore us to sanity. Values based on biblical truths gradually take hold in our lives.

When we surrender to God, we begin brain restoration anchored in love. Experiencing grace gradually improves vagal nerve tone, which leads to improved autonomic balance. With the help of our vagal nervous system, the fight, flight, or freeze sympathetic nervous system gradually stands down and our parasympathetic nervous system strengthens as our enteric nervous system settles down and provides the nutritional foundation necessary for health.

Surrender to God helps us restore emotional balance and eases our recovery from fear and anger. The wear and tear on our brain and heart of heightened sympathetic arousal is minimized. Cortisol levels fluctuate according to real short-term needs rather than getting stuck in response to chronic stress so we can become more emotionally and physically healthy.[305] The health benefits of a well-tuned autonomic nervous system begin to come about through a loving relationship with God.

When we are reminded in the throes of guilt, embarrassment, shame, or self-disgust that God understands our brokenness and loves us unconditionally, we can begin to see ourselves through God's eyes. The panic of abandoning our old selves that is triggering our sympathetic nervous system is down-regulated by the sensed safety of God's grace. As God uses our pain to move us closer to Him, the heat of corrective emotions begins to cool and we can consider our broken behavior constructively. This emotional response helps us test the limits of our values and move closer to the character of Jesus. Grace in the face of corrective emotions gives us the opportunity to refine our faithful brain fitness.

Of all the experiences available to us, pain is the least ambiguous and the most motivating. Considered this way, self-inflicted emotional trauma may have a purpose beyond the pain. This is especially important with corrosive shame, a mark of evil effectively countered by God's grace. The punishing self-blame of shame is ludicrous in the light of God's love, but we might accept it without question and make poor choices. The choice to follow Jesus is the only healthy antidote to shame. As my pastor says, "Jesus intervenes between God's holy justice and his steadfast love."[376] As we surrender to the new covenant love Jesus offers, the sting of shame begins to lessen and calms our self-disgust so we can begin to heal.

I have seen this in my own life and in the lives of thousands of my clients. As prideful people, we can inflict so much damage on ourselves that we become exhausted. When we come to the end of our own resources, all that's left is God's love.

"All that's left is God's love!" What a remarkable statement; full of hope if we have the faith to believe. Accepting God's amazing grace allows us to move through our pain as we struggle to let go of pride and self-sufficiency.

> Amazing Grace, how sweet the sound,
> That saved a wretch like me.
> I once was lost but now am found,
> Was blind, but now I see.
>
> 'Twas Grace that taught my heart to fear.
> And Grace, my fears relieved.
> How precious did that Grace appear
> The hour I first believed.
>
> Through many dangers, toils and snares
> I have already come;
> 'Tis Grace that brought me safe thus far
> and Grace will lead me home.
>
> When we've been there ten thousand years
> Bright shining as the sun.
> We've no less days to sing God's praise
> Than when we've first begun.[377]

Captain John Newton wrote the words that became the famous hymn in 1772 after a career on British slave ships, carrying captured humans from Africa to England. In the middle of an overpowering Atlantic storm, when his ship was about to sink, he surrendered to God. He admitted his depravity and began a gradual conversion. He entered a life devoted to God, eventually being ordained as a priest in the Church of England.

"Amazing Grace" became famous as the anthem of enslaved people in the American South, encouraging us to consider the humility of surrender to God's love as an antidote to the slavery of pride. We need to begin our recovery from prideful slavery by accepting that we're inherently inadequate. If we continue to believe in our adequacy, there's no need to surrender and ask for God's help.

Fortunately, after pursuing the American dream without God, I came to the end of my resources and was overwhelmed. I became depressed as I mourned the life apart from God that I had been living.

As it was for the apostle Peter and for John Newton, God's amazing gift of grace rescued me. On that Sunday morning in church more than thirty years ago, I began to actively explore the safety and freedom God's grace provides. Grace allowed me to face my ugly truth, admit my guilt, and start to get honest with God. Corrective emotions such as embarrassment and shame began to take their proper place in my life as God developed my faithful brain.

Chapter Takeaways

1. Embarrassment, shame, and disgust are corrective emotions triggered by guilt.
2. Corrective emotions arise when you're guilty of behaviors counter to your values.

3. Corrective emotions are processed in your brain's default mode network (DMN).
4. The DMN is the center of your conscience and personal morality.
5. Grace is the context for accepting the often-ugly truth about your behavior.
6. Grace helps corrective emotions to bring about healthy change.

Discussion Questions

1. What does experiencing God's grace do for your brain?
2. When was the last time you asked God for grace and forgiveness?
3. How does grace help you face the truth about yourself?
4. Are you ready to ask God to help you develop your faithful brain?

CHAPTER 9

A Faithful Brain Is Truth-Guided

I am the way and the truth and the life. No one comes to the Father except through me.

—*John 14:6*

Brain Basics

1. The truth you embrace is the foundation of your values.
2. Values influence your emotions and thoughts and persistently guide your behavior.
3. God-reflecting virtues are the basis of values that establish neural patterns that lead to the highest possible quality of life.

Whose Truth Is It?

In my young adulthood, I had strongly rejected this verse from the gospel of John and embraced the philosophy of Fritz Perls, summarized in this quotation: "I do my thing and you do your thing. I am not in this world to live up to your expectations, and you're not in this world to live up to mine. You are you, and I am I, and if by chance we find each other, it's beautiful. If not, it can't be helped."[378]

Perls developed Gestalt Therapy, an approach to psychotherapy that emphasized each person's unique experience as the core of his or her personal truth. Perls reflected the philosophical emphasis on the vitality of life experienced in every moment that had been described by Friedrich Nietzsche.

Dallas Willard, the chair of the School of Philosophy at the University of Southern California, compared the approaches to life offered by Nietzsche and Jesus, beginning with how each approached truth. He pointed out that Nietzsche has continued to have a powerful influence on American universities: "If you say 'truth' in most places on the college campuses I'm familiar with, people will immediately say 'Whose truth?'"[184]

From the perspective of Perls and Nietzsche, it makes sense to ask, "Whose truth is it?" because they hold that each of us has a unique experience of life and therefore a personal truth about reality. Rather than a universal truth, they would argue that my truth and your truth are unique to each of us.

In contrast, Willard argued that there is an ultimate truth that reflects God's created reality. Willard refers to this truth as "God's truth."[184]

Although living with personal truth may appear to be liberating because we needn't live up to each other's expectations, it literally stunts brain development. Your brain develops best in response to just-right challenges within the context of loving and respectful relationships. The developing brain's problem with the Perls and Nietzsche emphasis on individuality is that we need just-right interpersonal challenges for healthy brain development. If we each stay within the boundaries of our personal truth, we're likely to not develop sufficiently-challenging interpersonal relationships. As a consequence, brain development will be stunted.

The mutually nurturing relationships that foster optimal brain development must be worked out using principles that reflect God's created reality. The principles of Perls and Nietzsche are somewhat helpful because they correctly guide us to not live up to other people's expectations. But, "If not, it can't be helped" mistakenly avoids the mutual responsibility that challenging relationships require. The principles of Perls and Nietzsche would have us turn away from each other when the going gets tough, a regrettable mistake I made in marriage during early adulthood. Every good relationship is challenging and requires commitment and work because we're all broken in unique ways. Meeting the just-right challenges that arise as broken people come together requires a sound foundation of values based on a shared reality.

The fundamental problem is that we have difficulty accepting God's truth in place of our personal truth. We act according to our personal truth and at odds with God's truth. When we do, we move out of synchrony with God's created reality, creating problems for ourselves and others.

Jesus offers an alternative that reflects God's created reality. Jesus provides grace as the context within which our synchrony with God's truth can be examined. Jesus' way provides us with the opportunity to implement principles that produce growth as we live in synchrony with how our brains were designed. When we follow Jesus' way, we embrace God's truth and become free to fully engage with God's creation. Jesus' way provides a rich, vibrant opportunity to live that develops our brains optimally because our brains were designed to fully engage with God's creation. Growth occurs because Jesus' way offers the just-right challenge of facing God's truth within the safe context of God's love.

How Did You Embrace God's Truth?

I was helped to understand the opportunity Jesus offers when Pastor Rick Warren asked me to recite John 14:6 aloud: "I am the way and the truth and the life. No one comes to the Father except through me." After my recitation, his question astounded me. "Is Jesus making a threat or offering a promise?"

Wow! In my pride I had been taking it as a threat—take it or leave it! So I had left it, rejecting an opportunity to embrace Jesus' way and truth and life.

This experience shifted my thinking, and I began to explore the possibility that my way and truth and life were not as good as what Jesus offered. Being a scientist, I explored this with the tools of science, beginning with qualitative research on myself.

Science is based on the intertwined ideas that there's only one truth and we are to do our best to falsify it.[379] If, by observing the response to experimental manipulation, we can't disprove a theory that explains the observable facts, we are to accept the theory as a workable truth.

Although many people accept John 14:6 as truth, as a scientist at the start of my faith journey, I considered it as a testable theory. I began to test the theory that Jesus was the way and the truth and the life by experimenting with my life. I started my research with the observable fact that my choices affect my quality of life. If Jesus' way wasn't based on truth, my life should not have been affected by whether I chose or rejected the way of Jesus.

I found (and continue to find) that choosing or rejecting Jesus' way affects my quality of life. When I make choices inconsistent with the life and teachings of Jesus, I get bad results more often than when I make Jesus-way choices. I tested this (and sometimes still test this) by not following Jesus' way, which usually degrades my quality of life. Thank God for grace; I am a work in progress.

Does quality of life *always* degrade if I reject Jesus' way and *always* improve if I accept his way? No. In the short run, life continues to be as difficult as it was if I don't follow Jesus' way.

Doesn't that require that I falsify my theory? If I follow Jesus and life still sucks, aren't I just fooling myself? If there really is a relationship between following Jesus and improved quality of life, shouldn't life start to turn around once I make that choice?

Not necessarily, and to explain this, I need to give you a brief introduction to statistics. When one thing affects another thing, they are said to be correlated. Psychologists use statistics to determine whether a correlation is strong enough to be real because a correlation may be happening by chance. For example, in figure 8, we have sets of overlapping normal curves based on gender, comparing men and women.

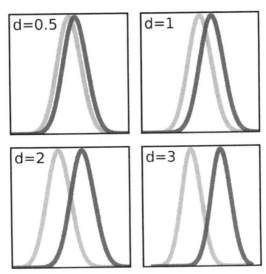

FIGURE 8. EFFECT SIZE CURVES

The $d = 0.5$ curves are almost completely overlapping. The statistic $d = 0.5$ indicates a slight difference in the effect of gender on attitudes about casual sex held by men and women; women have slightly more conservative views than men,[380] and there's a lot of overlap. In comparison, the curves for $d = 2$ represents the effect of gender on lift capacity;[381] most men can lift more than most women, and there's only a little overlap. What is known as "effect size" is an estimate of the power of a phenomenon—how much something affects what we're measuring.

Many human characteristics appear to be related but are actually not related; the appearance of a relationship is based on chance. Statistics help us sort out the chance correlations from the real correlations; the greater the effect size, the more likely the correlation is real and not just due to chance.

For several years, I tested my theory on the irrelevance of Jesus, looking for examples in my own life that would prove that Jesus' way wasn't the true way, but the correlation was just too strong. The power of Jesus' way compared with my way was too great, exceeding $d = 3$ in my experience. When I started to follow Jesus, my quality of life gradually improved; not with every choice I made, but with many of them.

But wait a minute. That still didn't allow me to attribute to Jesus my improved quality of life; there may have been another cause.

That was possibly true. I saw a strong correlation between choosing Jesus' way and my improved quality of life, but I couldn't prove cause and effect. But I also no longer believed that the pattern and frequency of my choices leading to improved quality of life were coincidences due only to chance. Some may be due to chance, but many coincidences in my life align along a pathway that leads me to God, which requires faith in a universal reality with which I could align my choices. At these times, Jesus' way and truth and my life seemed to be linked.

How Are Jesus' Way and Truth and Life Linked?

I think of these as intertwined in the character of Jesus. It's a workable truth that neuroplasticity causes what we do to affect who we become, our character. And we know our character affects what we do; character is revealed in the patterns of our behaviors. But the relationship between character and behavior is not simply circular; it's a spiral over time. None of us has a trajectory of growth that is a straight line up or down; we spiral like a corkscrew around the pivot point of the truth we embrace.

I also noticed that my quality of life tended to follow the corkscrew trajectory of character growth. When I started to make the person and teaching of Jesus central to my life, my quality-of-life corkscrew trajectory began to curve upward. Over time, I can look back at the trajectory and see that the current bottom of my quality of life tends to be higher than most of my earlier tops.

In community with other Jesus followers, I can report that as we follow the way and truth of Jesus, we gradually adopt his character. His way becomes our personal path to God's truth: we're designed to have what he called "life to the full" (John 10:10).

In the brain, accepting and embracing God's truth leads to the development of values such as honesty, integrity, respect for others, and the importance of fairness and forgiveness.[1] Values are represented in very elaborate neural patterns that begin in the limbic system and extend up throughout the cerebral cortex. The limbic system is where our emotions originate, directly below the cerebral cortex. Neural patterns of values trigger emotions that influence the development of thoughts that in turn guide the development of neural networks that embody our beliefs and goals and attitudes. In turn, beliefs and goals and attitudes guide our choices.

Without values, we're left with only desire to guide us, with predictably poor results. Desire is driven by brief and often powerful neurochemical eruptions. Desire powerfully guides the brain moment to moment, without any future perspective, and is devoid of responsibility. The risk-taking that adolescents engage in is a prime example of desire-driven behavior. We now understand that the incomplete development of the adolescent brain leaves allows it to be the victim of desire-driven behavior.[382-386]

So the truth that we embrace is the foundation of our values. Early on, as I embraced my narrow truth of the American dream, my values focused on desire for beauty, power, wealth, and independence. I worshipped these, and they defined what I now recognize was an impoverished quality of life. Beauty, power, wealth, and independence are attractive qualities, but they don't necessarily coincide with Jesus' way. I don't have an easy answer for how to integrate these into a life devoted to Jesus, but I can report I didn't handle it well. As I became "successful," I found myself moving away from the Jesus of my childhood. God gradually became inconvenient, an impediment to my participation in the Southern California lifestyle.

Years later, after I crashed and burned, I began to examine the shallow truth on which I had built my early adulthood values. I learned that the core of Christianity on which biblical truths are based is God's love. "Love the Lord your God with all your heart and soul and mind ... love your neighbor as yourself." For me, I must love God first because God's grace is the context within which I can love my new Jesus-way-and-truth–infused self and become ready to love my neighbor.

Truth in the context of grace exemplified by Jesus brought me back to John 14:6: "I am the way and the truth and the life." And instead of just any values, I began to think about the idea of *God-reflecting virtues* that helped me develop God-reflecting values. I interpret these virtues as ideal principles and standards of behavior that align with God's created reality.

Your brain was designed to operate best in synchrony with God's creation, so following these virtues to develop your values aligns your brain with God's created reality, which allows your brain to develop optimally.

Where Do We Find God-Reflecting Virtues?

God-reflecting virtues are the essence of the biblical narrative of Jesus' way and truth and life. Studying the Bible and other books that explain the Bible, listening to Bible scholars and pastors explain the lessons of Jesus, and sharing thoughts and ideas with other Jesus followers help these virtues develop the values that guide our lives. Here is a simple depiction of how truth plays out in my brain.

Biblical Truths and Virtues > Values > Beliefs and Attitudes > Choices and Goals

Based on biblical truths and virtues, my values lead to beliefs and attitudes that persistently guide my choices and goals. These choices determine my behavior and show up as my character. The Bible is my ever-available source of truth, virtues, and values resulting in behavior that reflects the character of Jesus.

An important point is that my attitudes are shaped by the virtues and values I embrace. Attitudes are closely linked to the limbic system, our emotional brain, which puts them out of the direct reach of logic and reason.[156-158] It's not that attitudes cannot be accessed; it's just that we must influence them through our values, which are found above the limbic system, in the prefrontal area of the cerebral cortex. For example, belief in God is necessary, but Jesus asks us to go further and develop a trusting relationship with him. Many people believe in God but don't have the faith to trust God to guide their lives; recall Carol in chapter 3 and Charlie in chapter 4.

Faith comes from the choice to accept Jesus' invitation to follow him and fully embrace biblical truths and virtues. Faith in the truth and virtue of God gradually helps us develop values that reflect the character of Jesus and synchronizes our behaviors with God's created reality.

Our research at the Faithful Brain Institute examines the patterns of character development by Christians, using Jesus as the standard, based on universal character traits. [122] We ask people to compare themselves to Jesus because the reliability and validity of self-ratings is dependent on a clear standard.[387] As a universal standard of character, Jesus is an obvious choice because he is so well known and is widely viewed as a person of unquestionable character. Please consider participating in this research. Participation is voluntary and results in free information you will find useful. To participate, go to the "Research" page at www.faithfulbrain.com.

How Does Character Affect Us?

Character is the consistent behavioral presentation of your underlying values, how you're known. Character is what others can expect of you. The Boy Scouts' motto, "Character counts," reflects an ideal supported in research on success.[122, 388-390] People who develop into successful leaders have stable, enduring character traits their colleagues and followers are able to identify, appreciate, and embrace.[391-394] The consistency of a person's character is directly tied to the clarity of that person's values and the moral courage he or she demonstrates.

Character develops rapidly over the first twenty-five years of life and seems to become localized in the prefrontal cortex of the brain by that age. Our parents begin our character development by modeling and guiding the development of our temperament, even before we have language to understand their words. In middle childhood, temperament begins to coalesce into character, guided by many influential adults. Children who don't have such influence or who are influenced by adults whose character is counter to the prevailing social values have a more difficult time in adolescence and do less well in transitioning to adulthood. The character traits of women tend to stabilize somewhat earlier than the character traits of men, reflecting different rates of brain development. Character development continues to be possible throughout life, but only with intention and dedication to aligning one's behavior with a consistent set of values.

Our character affects all we do. There are two intertwined primary effects that can be ascribed to character.

1. The degree to which we have achieved stability of character influences the organization of our brain and the efficiency of our cognitive processing. When we have

well-developed character, our beliefs are consistent with our attitudes, which align our behaviors. Because this will not always lead to behavior that help us love our neighbor as ourselves, we need a standard of character development that helps us grow in that direction. Jesus' way provides that standard and the opportunity for gradual development of character as we follow his path.

2. The degree to which our character is synchronized with prevailing social values will influence our friendships and other relationships, our success at school and work, our earning capacity, our likelihood of incarceration, and even how long we will live. These effects occur to the extent that we are participating in our social milieu. If our character fits within the prevailing social norms, we can participate and gradually hone our character without needing to make major changes. On the other hand, if our character is misfit, we will marginalize ourselves. We might even need to be incarcerated because the prevailing social norms must be maintained and protected from our behaviors. The misfit problem points to the importance of Jesus as the standard for both individual and cultural character development.

This leads us to a discussion about the optimal context for character development, which is the most important issue facing every modern society and the topic of the next chapter.

Chapter Takeaways

1. The truth you embrace is the foundation of your values.
2. Values influence your emotions and thoughts and persistently guide your behavior.

3. God's truth and God-reflecting virtues are the basis of values that establish neural patterns based on the highest standards that lead to the highest quality-of-life possible.

Discussion Questions

1. How does modeling yourself after Jesus develop your character in today's world?
2. What can you do in the next week to further develop values consistent with God's truth?
3. Comparing your character when you were sixteen with your character now, are there any differences? If there are differences, how did they develop?

CHAPTER 10

A Faithful Brain Is Organized by God

I am the way and the truth and the life. **No one comes to the Father except through me.**

—*John 14:6*

Brain Basics

1. Values help develop and maintain brain efficiency and organization.
2. Poorly developed values contribute to brain chaos and confusion.
3. Strong values can be "wrong" values.
4. Jesus' values are synchronized with God's created reality.
5. Free will is an opportunity to test and develop our values with the help of corrective emotions.

"No one comes to the Father except through me" means that we must always defer moral authority to Jesus. Bible-based morality requires us to get beyond our self-justified beliefs, attitudes, and opinions and focus on his example of love and grace. None of us ever has the moral high ground because

Jesus always has the moral higher ground. "What would Jesus do?" can be a useful question because it synchronizes our alignment with God's created reality. "No one comes to the Father except through me" is Jesus' promise that his way and truth align us with God's created reality. It's a promise within which we can relax and drop our petty differences so that God can develop us in his likeness.

Unfortunately, in the busyness of modern life, many of us have defaulted to moral rules and don't fully consider Jesus' way and truth when we make decisions. We like shortcuts that save fifteen seconds here and thirty seconds there. Moral rules are habits that save time and are sometimes useful but always oversimplify our values. They're cognitively efficient and help us keep our brains organized, but they can usually benefit from examination. This is why it's a good idea to be part of a community in which members challenge each other to look at how well our values align with Jesus' way and truth and life. Cognitive efficiency and organization are basic design parameters of your brain, but they're the tail wagging the dog when it comes to morality.

Why Are Cognitive Efficiency and Brain Organization Important?

Your brain is designed to conserve its resources. Although it's only 2 percent of your body mass, it uses 20 to 25 percent of your total body energy.[395] Inefficiency and disorganization waste brain energy.

The young adult brain has about 100 billion neurons, each with between 1,000 and 30,000 connections to other neurons, plus about 900 billion support cells.[396] If we consider only the minimum number of connections for all 100 billion neurons, the number of possible neuronal connections in the brain is at least 1×10^{14}, that is, 100 trillion. If we consider the number of possible patterns and combination of patterns in the brain, the potential connections quickly balloon *beyond* astronomical numbers. In fact, scientists not only don't know how many connections are possible in the human brain, it's also more than we can measure! We are created in the image of God.

This is very humbling for us scientists because we try to measure everything. Anything that's beyond our ability to measure makes us uncomfortable. I made some of my professional colleagues uncomfortable when I invented *Godzillion,* to indicate that only God can grasp this beyond-measurement aspect of our being.

> **Godzillion**
> The uncountable number of possible neural patterns and combinations in the human brain.

And then we have to consider how *quickly* the brain operates. To give you an idea of this, let's compare the number of operations occurring in your brain per second with the number of operations that occur in a supercomputer. Estimates such as these are now being avoided by scientists because each estimate seems to be exceeded by the next estimate as we learn more about the brain. The most recent published estimate I can find is from 2009, when the Director of Cognitive Computing at IBM reported[397] that the human brain performs approximately 38,000 trillion operations per second and can hold about 3,584 terabytes of memory.[8]

How big a number is 38,000 trillion? Let's say that you could tap your finger ten times each second, which is faster than you can tap, but let's start there. How long would it take

---

[8] The Hubble Space Telescope collected forty-five terabytes of data in its first twenty years of observations, one-eightieth of your brain's capacity.

you to tap your finger 38,000 trillion times? If you start right now, you would be finished tapping your finger 120,414,734 years from now!

Go ahead, get started. I'll wait in the car.

All done? I'll bet you're tired. I'm tired just thinking about it. But your brain handles 38,000 trillion operations *per second* for every second of your life. And then, in the next second, some of the neural patterns change!

Beyond these changes inside your brain, your brain efficiently integrates the flow of information outside the brain with your body and with other brains.[360] Your neurochemicals and hormones excite some brain mechanisms or calm others and cause genetic switches to be turned on or off, creating complexity beyond comprehension.

This is where the reality of the soul becomes crucially important in discussions of faith and neuroscience. I think of the soul as representing the potential into which we have the opportunity to grow our relational brains, using free will properly. The necessarily unlimited nature of the soul's capacity gives me confidence that science can never fully grasp God's created reality. This realization helped me to surrender to God; I hope my brothers and sisters in the scientific community can experience something similar.

A God-dedicated soul is necessary because godzillions of opportunities for chaos and confusion are always present in our brains. For decades, one of the main arguments against neuroplasticity was that it would create chaos in our brains. The rhetorical question asked by scientists and philosophers opposed to the idea of neuroplasticity was, "How can an organism that is so complex avoid chaos and confusion if it's constantly changing?" Part of the answer comes from the agency of values and their effect on chaos and confusion.

Confusion will stop your brain from doing its best to take care of you. The most immediate characteristic of people who remain conscious after a brain injury is confusion. When a football player comes off the field after a hard hit, we ask these questions to begin screening for a brain injury.

- Where are you?
- Which half is it?
- Who scored last?
- What team did we play last?
- Did we win the last game?

What we're looking for is confusion due to concussion, which occurs when neural patterns have been damaged. Cognitive confusion means that the athlete's brain can't take care of the athlete, who is immediately benched and put in sensory isolation so the harmful neurochemical cascade triggered by the concussion can subside.[398, 399] Cognitive confusion is important, but the ultimate confusion involves our values.

Why Is Values Confusion So Important?

Values provide the neural framework for organizing information as it comes in and for consolidating ideas and memories as they're forming. Values guide our attention and filter what we understand, causing our emotional responses to certain situations to be sensitized. Values help our thinking to remain organized.

When a person comes into my office in deep emotional pain, the most common cause is values confusion. Whether caused by a conflict of their values with another person or by a traumatic event that has turned his or her world upside down, values confusion is a serious problem. The person is not thinking clearly and is more likely to make poor or even dangerous choices. When you're confused, your brain is not fully capable of taking care of you, and you need to be benched.

Values confusion is very painful because it strikes at who we are, at our core. "I knew better than that, but I just wanted to see what would happen" or "I can't believe they fired me for something silly like that, after all I've done for them" or "I don't know why I blew up like that; I just went crazy" are all sincere statements from recent clients, stemming from their values confusion. Values confusion threatens who we want to be so painfully that it can lead even to suicide or homicide.

Strong values help us avoid values confusion and maintain brain organization and efficiency. As information comes into our brain, strong values help us efficiently organize it into consistent neural patterns. As long as the information is consistent with our values, it's easily organized and we experience understanding. But if the information doesn't square with our values, it starts to create confusion. When we have strong values, we aren't as easily confused if we have a serious conflict with others' values. Strong values help us avoid the discomfort of confusion and maintain our integrity under pressure to conform to others' values.

Let's take a look at how having strong values applies to your life. In this example, you're walking on a cold, wintry street behind an elderly person who, without noticing, drops a $20 bill on the sidewalk. You pick it up and in one second decide to give it back to the person.

In that second, you had at least two competing thoughts each based on values that have developed over the course of your lifetime. Just like a hurricane gradually organizes over time from the chaos of trillions of diverse inputs, your values have gradually organized over time from trillions of diverse inputs.

And I'll bet your values seem to you to be coherent rather than chaotic. How can that be? How did you move from a huge number of inputs to having coherent value patterns in your brain that allowed you to quickly make a simple comparison between putting the $20 in your pocket and giving it back to the elderly person?

I ask because I want to point out that we must develop and maintain coherent values so our brains don't become chaotic. Our values allow us to put the $20 in our pocket or give it back. We aren't forced to do one or the other; we can make a choice.

Values-based choosing is what theologians call free will, a basic brain process that's always occurring. Exercising free will allows us to grow and further develop our faithful brain by testing our values. We choose based on our values, and the act of choosing develops our character, shaped by our corrective emotions. This is the character-development process that makes each of us more unique than our fingerprints. C. S. Lewis wrote,

> If a thing is free to be good it is also free to be bad. And free will is what has made evil possible. Why, then, did God give them free will? Because free will, though it makes evil possible, is also the only thing that makes possible any love or goodness or joy worth having.[345]

From my point of view, as I consider how to help people develop faithful brains, free will allows us opportunities to shape our character. In the process of making wrong choices, we encounter corrective emotions that cause us to change course and examine our character. This is such an important process that it must be directed by the best values available, which is why Jesus' values are so important.

Why Are Jesus' Values So Important?

Because your brain can avoid confusion with any strong values based on whatever truth you embrace, the truth you embrace is crucial. Strong values can be wrong values *almost* as easily as they can be right values. We can identify people in history such as Hitler and Stalin who had strong values that were wrong values. Their strong values powerfully organized their brains, leading to policies and action resulting in mass murder and genocide.

Malignant values are widely available and expressed in less-virulent forms in our ethnic prejudices. Jesus didn't value skin color or accents or one gender over the other. Every choice along Jesus' way helped his truth shape our values, leading to life to the full. Organized by Jesus' values, our brain's organization becomes synchronized with God's created reality.

The basic idea is that by following Jesus' way, we develop neural patterns of values that reflect his character. This organizes our brain so we can think, act, and love with humility, purpose, and clarity.

In addition, adopting Jesus' values allows our brain to become more resilient. As principles and standards of behavior, Jesus' values are self-organizing mechanisms that help avoid brain chaos. A chaos theorist would say that Jesus' values become the "primary attractor"[400] in a potentially chaotic system, organizing neural networks to recognize complex patterns. Jesus' values allow us to harmonize with the rest of God's creation and grow closer to the Father.

Jesus' way also helps to orchestrate the potential chaos of *interacting* brains, for example, men and women in marriage. To the degree we can share his values in marriage, we keep both brains synchronized to help each spouse maintain brain efficiency and organization. New-covenant love-guided marriages demonstrate this constantly. My most recent disagreement with Mary was more easily resolved because we share basic values based on Jesus' way and truth.

How Can I Know I'm Following Jesus?

Go back to our $20 example; you can test whether you've been following Jesus by putting the $20 in your pocket. Within a few seconds, your brain reacts to this by triggering emotions that make you feel guilty or lucky, depending on the values that have been shaping your beliefs, goals, and attitudes. If you feel guilty but want the money and are willing to pay the price of the corrective emotions of embarrassment or shame, you keep the $20. But if the guilt or embarrassment or shame is not worth $20, you catch up to the elderly person and give it back.

But what if you notice that the person is of a different ethnic group? Will that affect your behavior? Of course it will. In addition to learning over the course of your lifetime to tell right from wrong, you've developed biases for and against people based on their ethnicity.

What if you notice the person is wearing a $2,000 overcoat? Will that affect your behavior? Of course it will. In addition to learning over the course of your lifetime to tell right from wrong, you've developed biases for or against wealthy people.

But what if you notice the old man's overcoat is tattered and dirty and he's wearing worn-out shoes without socks on this cold winter day? Will that affect your behavior? Of course it will. In addition to learning over the course of your lifetime to tell right from wrong, you have developed biases for and against homeless people.

I could go on and on, presenting different scenarios that are all reasonable and will figure into your deciding whether to keep the $20 or give it back all based on your values. The point to these scenarios is that your brain is organized by your values, your primary mechanism for avoiding confusion. Values always depend on the way you choose to follow and the truth you choose to embrace.

How Can I Get Started?

We need to open ourselves up to a relationship with Jesus and begin to pray, study the Bible, and participate actively in healthy communities of faith. Our trajectory will not be smoothly upward but will trace a spiral around which our lives revolve with God in the center. To borrow the title of Richard Rohr's wonderful book,[401] we'll begin "falling upward" into the beautiful future God has for each of us.

Prayer primes our neural patterns[374] through an invitation to the Holy Spirit. I don't understand the mystery of this, but my experience is that my prayers of surrender engage my entire being - heart, soul, strength, and mind - to such an extent that my intertwined thoughts and feelings are clarified by values not yet wholly my own.

Neuroconsolidation
Automatic, values-based neuronal pruning that brings personal truth to conscious awareness.

As I surrender, *neuroconsolidation* occurs, the organization of my experiences into long-term memories.[402] From my brain perspective, neuronal pruning shapes and sharpens my values as I quiet down and allow the Holy Spirit to work. These Ah ha! or enlightenment moments come unexpectedly, sometimes several times each day, and seem to be improved by brain-restorative sleep. Awakening with clarity and a flood of Ah ha! moments helps me appreciate that my sleep has been restorative.

How can I know my Ah ha! moments are trustworthy? I test these against what I learn in the Bible and by checking with my accountability partners. Studying the Bible provides the wisdom we need as we learn to live new lives. Bible scholars can provide guidance, and pastors can help us apply the ancient lessons of the Bible to our busy, modern lives. Our friends can encourage patience as we wrestle with ideas that sometimes are countercultural.

A healthy church community is an excellent environment for values development and consolidation. Relationships with people who are pursuing a relationship with God are necessary; our brains develop best in healthy community. In my church community, the neuroscience of faithful brain worship is captured with three related methods.

- We *explore* our relationship with God, engaging our left brain with the Bible and pastoral instruction; we can expand on Bible lessons with related literature, often in small study groups.
- We *experience* our relationship with God, engaging our right brain with worship music and songs linked to pastoral instruction and by developing transparent trust-relationships with others.

- We *express* our relationship with God by working in the community and in the greater world as we practice implementing our developing values and obedience to God.

The "three E's" help explain our approach to Christian life and community. This fits nicely with how Malcolm Jeeves and Warren Brown[88] described spirituality as involving "*experience* in terms of our awareness of the transcendent; *beliefs* in terms of what we believe about God, about ourselves, and about the world in which we live; and *action* in terms of how we live our lives." (emphasis mine)

Following Jesus toward the development of faithful brain fitness helps us live life to the full. As we practice following Jesus, our values begin as ideas we can consider and then test. Free will allows active consideration, which leads to partial adoption, which leads to further testing. As this process repeats, neuroplasticity gradually creates neural patterns of values that permeate the brain. As faithful brain development continues, Jesus' virtues and values seem to automatically guide our behaviors below our conscious awareness.

We become attuned to the Holy Spirit as we make ourselves available to God. This experience harnesses our neuroplasticity to develop our character to gradually reflect the character of Jesus. Through Jesus, we're offered the way and truth and life that lead to God. As we surrender and move towards God's perfect will for our lives, we get caught up in his created reality. To the degree that we can persist in our surrender and let God in to organize our neural networks with Jesus's values, our brains have the capacity to sample the magnificence of God's created reality.

Chapter Takeaways

1. The truth you embrace is the foundation of your values.
2. Values influence your emotions and thoughts and persistently guide your behavior.
3. Values help develop and maintain your brain's organization.
4. Poorly developed values allow chaos and confusion.
5. Free will is an opportunity to test and develop your values with the help of corrective emotions.
6. God-reflecting virtues are the basis of values that establish neural patterns based on the highest standards.

Discussion Questions

1. Has there been a time in your life when you didn't have clear, strong values?
2. What are your favorite moral rules? Why might they be insufficient?
3. Do you have someone who helps you explore your values and morality?
4. How will developing a more faithful brain help you experience a more productive, resilient, and meaningful life?

CHAPTER 11

A Faithful Brain Is Intentional

Therefore, I urge you, brothers and sisters, in view of God's mercy, to offer your bodies as a living sacrifice, holy and pleasing to God—this is your true and proper worship. Do not conform to the pattern of this world, but be transformed by the renewing of your mind. Then you will be able to test and approve what God's will is—his good, pleasing and perfect will.

—Romans 12:1–2

Brain Basics

1. We begin to develop a faithful brain by adopting the character of Jesus.
2. Contemplation of heaven is serenity in the brain; joy is its predominant feeling.
3. Prayer, studying the Bible, and participating in healthy communities of faith help us develop faithful brains.
4. Learning about brain structure and function compliments our spiritual development.

"... a living sacrifice, holy and pleasing to God"?

Saul of Tarsus was one of the least likely people to become a living sacrifice who was holy and pleasing to God. A zealous and dangerous enemy of Jesus' followers, his brain was transformed by his encounter with Jesus and he became the author of the words above. His brain transformation began when Jesus appeared to Saul as he traveled to Damascus after Jesus' resurrection. He was knocked to the ground and blinded. Jesus spoke to Saul and sent him on to Damascus to await further orders. After Saul had spent three days in Damascus, blind and without food or water, Jesus sent to him a frightened follower named Ananias.

> Placing his hands on Saul, he said, "Brother Saul, the Lord—Jesus, who appeared to you on the road as you were coming here—has sent me so that you may see again and be filled with the Holy Spirit." Immediately, something like scales fell from Saul's eyes, and he could see again. He got up and was baptized, and after taking some food, he regained his strength. (Acts 9:17-18)

Saul thereafter used his Roman name, Paul, and began to develop a faithful brain by adopting the character of Jesus. Neuroplasticity, neurogenesis, and neural epigenesis were all harnessed to transform his brain so that he became a great leader of the early Christian church, extending it far beyond the Jewish community of its roots. He was the first international evangelist, and he wrote much of the New Testament to encourage and guide Jesus followers, offering his transformation as an example to others.

Paul is also an excellent example for us because he is so transparent about his brokenness and its painful effects in his own life, as he wrote in his letter to the Christian community in Rome.

> I do not understand what I do. What I want to do I do not do, but what I hate I do ... I have the desire to do what is good, but I cannot carry it out. I do not do the good I want to do, but the evil I do not want to do—this I keep on doing. (Romans 7:15–19)

Paul seemed to understand that what we now know as neuroplasticity, neurogenesis, and neural epigenesis are mechanisms by which we can develop our good habits as well as "the evil I do not want to do."

As I look back on my early adulthood, I was a lot like Saul, an angry and zealous anti-theist. I was doing my best to try to debunk God and make fun of religious practices and anyone who espoused the Christian faith. I didn't know it then, but God was placing in my life people who eventually would draw me back to Jesus, including Danny Munday.

What Do You Want Most out of Life?

I met Danny Munday on Ward 905 at Rancho Los Amigos Hospital on the first day of my career, February 3, 1970. I had walked into the nursing station after the patients' breakfast and was greeted by Nurse Marci Worthington. Marci introduced me to Danny, a redhead boy with green eyes and a huge smile made all the more startling by its placement atop a tiny body shrunk by spinal muscular atrophy, an advancing and always fatal neuromuscular disorder.

"Hi, I'm Danny," he gurgled.

Calmly handing me a soft rubber hose, Marci showed me how to guide it down Danny's tracheostomy tube to suction mucous from his lungs. Danny could just barely breathe. Death from suffocation was part of Danny's constant reality. His gurgling was caused by mucous that would suffocate him if it weren't removed promptly.

FIGURE 9. DANNY MUNDAY

As Danny sat in his wheelchair and looked up at me, his smile and bright green eyes patiently allowing Marci to guide my clumsy hands to pull death from his lungs, I was introduced to the fragility of life.

At first, meeting Danny just reinforced the idea that God lets bad things happen to good people. This was my main objection to Christianity when I walked away from God a few years before. If God is all powerful and lets bad things to happen to good people, why should we love God at all, let alone with all our heart and soul and strength and mind?

I didn't recognize until much later that God had anticipated my question, placing in my life many good people to whom bad things had happened. If I paid attention to how *they* were learning to live life to the full, they would help me understand.

Danny helped me appreciate that outside of critical care hospital rooms or in active combat, we aren't normally aware that death is our constant companion. But several times each day, mucous would cause Danny to struggle for breath. Whenever this happened, he had a few minutes to live. In between, he lived with joy, pursuing goals that made life worth living.

Through Danny, I was introduced to the potential for joy up close to death. Many people don't know that joy is even a possibility when death is close. Getting close to death cancels their joy and brings only despair. But it didn't for Danny. Joy was what Danny wanted most out of life.

What Is Joy?

Joy is the designed state of a faithful brain, fully integrated with God, within itself and with others. Joy erupts as we're fully engaged in the moment. If we're well loved and cared for, we experience joy often when we are young. Joy is the usual state of a faithful brain when we surrender to God. Unfortunately it's hard to grasp this simple truth and we spend much unnecessary time, attention, and capital pursuing joy.

FIGURE 10. JOY!

The Oxford English Dictionary defines joy as depending on our circumstances and is "the emotion evoked by well-being, success, or good fortune or by the prospect of possessing what one desires."[403] From this perspective, joy would increase or decrease as our circumstances improved or deteriorated.

For Danny and all my clients with fatal illnesses or serious disabilities, this is absolutely unacceptable. If joy depended on "well-being, success, or good fortune," my clients would never be joyful. Danny was the first of thousands of people who have taught me that this is a lie, and research conducted at Rancho and the Faithful Brain Institute confirms its falsity. [178] As my good friend Bryan Kemp says, "Once you have the basic needs met, improving your standard of living doesn't improve your quality of life. What we need most is a purpose in life that's greater than our circumstances."

Searching for joy in our circumstances is a fool's errand. Basing joy on our circumstances is an attempt to be independent from God, when joy actually is a consequence of our ability to safely rest in God. C. S. Lewis wrote, "Joy is the serious business of Heaven."[404] For Lewis, me, and many others, joy flows from dependence on Jesus, who guarantees our relationship with God. But some of us then take God for granted and lose our joy. Lewis writes that we need reminders.

> When we are lost in the woods the sight of a signpost is a great matter. He who first sees it cries, "Look!" The whole party gathers round and stares. But when we have found the road and are passing signposts every few miles, we shall not stop and stare.[405]

Lewis considered joy as a signpost that points to God. Joy pulls us out of the dark woods toward the light of God's love. Our relationship with God brings us joy as the "peace that passes all understanding" that Paul described in his letter to the Philippians.

Kay Warren's definition of joy is very helpful to me; I use it daily with myself and my clients. Warren defines joy as "the settled assurance that God is in control of all the details of my life, the quiet confidence that ultimately everything is going to be alright, and the determined choice to praise God in every situation."[406] She writes that "Joy is a choice" we must make in spite of our circumstances. Depending on God to be in control of the details of life allows us to not be dependent on our circumstances. Joy is our brain's natural response when we're closer to God than we are to our circumstances.

How Can I Find Joy in Difficult Circumstances?

But "everything is going to be alright"? For me and Saddleback Church founders Rick and Kay Warren and so many others, Jesus makes joy available in tough times. The Warrens lost their son Matthew to mental illness in 2013; his suicide was tragic and very painful, but I am confident his family has "the quiet confidence that ultimately everything is going to be alright." Here is what Kay shared with the Saddleback Church community several months after Matthew's death.

> I was wearing a necklace that says "Choose Joy." After I wrote that several years ago, I wrote the book because I struggled with low levels of depression my whole life. Yet here's a verse like Romans 5:3-5 that says, "We can have joy even in our troubles because we know these troubles produce endurance. And endurance produces character, and character produces hope. And this hope will not disappoint us, because God has poured his love to fill our hearts."
>
> I began to look for some jewelry that I could wear on a daily basis to remind me that I could choose joy, that there could be joy even in troubles.
>
> The day that Matthew passed away, as Rick said, I had a terrible sense of foreboding. I had very good reasons to believe that he had taken his life. But we had to wait hours before it could be confirmed.
>
> When I got up that morning I deliberately went to my jewelry box and with my hands shaking and my heart pounding and my stomach heaving I

picked this necklace out of the jewelry box. I wasn't really thinking very clearly. But I knew that by putting it on in some way I was fighting back against the nightmare that I was pretty sure was going to unfold that day.

As we stood at Matthew's house together waiting for the police to confirm this terrible news, I don't know why but in a moment I looked down and saw it and then I raised it to him in a very tiny feeble attempt to affirm what I knew to be the truth. Even when, as Rick said, our hearts were shattering.

How could I do that? How could I even wear the necklace that day? How could I lift it to him in a gesture of belief in God? A belief that joy can be chosen even in our darkest moments. How could I do that? And how could he through his tears receive it and not push me away and not tell me I was crazy and to stop it, and not do that?

It's because of what we know. Because we know that joy is still present. We know it, because God is good. And because we have spent the last fifty years of our lives putting our spiritual roots down deep into the rich soil of God's grace, his mercy, his faithfulness and his goodness. And because of that, because of those roots that have gone deep into the soil of who God is, getting to know him, when troubles have come our way we have been able to produce endurance. It has been produced. And hopefully character. And from that character, hope and joy.

Verse 5 from Romans 5 again, look at that, "And this hope will not disappoint us, because God has poured his love to fill our hearts."

I was learning a lot about joy in the last few years so I could say, "Yes God, I trust you and I'm going to have joy even in this very dark day."[407]

Joy is a life-affirming experience that arises from our surrender to God. Relying on God so we can choose joy is especially important in difficult times. We don't become free of problems when we follow Jesus; I have fewer problems caused by my self-centeredness, but my life still has many challenges. The difference is that when life goes other than how I had planned, I interpret the new direction as God's will and try to use the challenge to grow.

I often don't know God's precise purpose for my life, but I have quiet confidence that ultimately everything will be alright. I now take my ongoing challenges as signposts that I am to follow rather than as fear-inducing. I have the settled assurance and quiet confidence that there's deeper meaning in these challenges. As I seek their deeper meaning, I sometimes find it, and more often, I find joy.

The way this seems to work is to accept our circumstances as the reality that we must face rather than wishing life were different. This is a perspective we can develop. My clients and I approach cancer, heart disease, paralysis, brain damage, amputations, blindness, mental illness, and progressive neurologic diseases with the quiet confidence that everything is going to be alright. Danny was the first of several thousand people who taught me this lesson.

How Did Danny Teach You about Joy?

During evenings at the hospital, after he had finished therapy and school, Danny and I would find a quiet corner and have serious conversations about life. I have a favorite question I ask seriously ill children: "I know you don't really believe in magic, but if you had a magic wand, what would you do with it?" I am looking for one of two answers. Some children tell me they would use their magic wand to walk again or to cure their illness. Others tell me they want more friends or to visit Disneyland. The first group of kids is struggling with the reality of their lives; the second group has begun to transcend their reality and negotiate with life on life's terms.

When I asked Danny my magic wand question, he quickly answered, "To kiss Jane Fonda," which definitely put Danny in the second group. He had a movie poster of Ms. Fonda as "Barbarella" tacked to the ceiling above his bed.

Did you just say, "How useless! What a foolish goal. Kissing Jane Fonda when he's got a fatal illness? Why waste time with foolishness like that?"

The first part of the answer to your question about wasting time is that we don't know how much time we have left, even when we're as sick as Danny. The second part of the answer to your question is that meaningful goals can lead to optimism, which gives us more time on this planet because optimism improves our health.[408-410] Our immune system is healthier, our stress responses calm down, and depression is avoided or resolved by optimism. Neuroplasticity, neurogenesis, and neural epigenesis unfold more dependably when we're optimistic. Our brain is literally energized as we move toward meaningful goals,[411-413] and problems with stress and depression can be more easily resolved. Given the detrimental effects of stress and depression on the brain, meaningful goals can be brain-protective.

The third part of the answer is that meaningful goals pursued with optimism pull us into a valued future.[414] Danny's goal to kiss Jane Fonda linked him to a valued future. Time and again, with thousands of terminally ill and severely disabled clients, I have seen goals pull the person into an unexpectedly bright future. Having something to live for helps each day become valuable and encourages our engagement in life.

The final part of the answer is that pursuing goals toward a valued future in the face of apparently overwhelming obstacles can remind us that we need God. Think about this for a moment; I don't want you to miss it. If you have never experienced paralysis or overwhelming pain, it's very hard to understand. Because Danny's paralysis was almost total, it was obvious that he was dependent on others. This created appreciation for those who cared for him that grew into love. And beyond his dependence on others, it was vitally important to Danny to depend on God, for whom his appreciation also grew into love.

Why Was Danny's Dependence on God Important?

The answer is simple: God is completely dependable and people aren't. Danny could experience joy in spite of his circumstances because he trusted God. Danny expected that whatever awaited him would be worthy of that trust. He welcomed God's presence in his life.

Danny taught me that disability can be a valuable opportunity if it expands our ability to become comfortable with dependence. Overwhelming pain and terminal illness offer similar opportunities.

At first, the thought of becoming comfortable with dependence sounded so strange to me that I couldn't believe it. Dependence is difficult for me, just as it is for many people. Many of us pretend we're completely independent in spite of plenty of evidence to the contrary. We struggle to project an image of independence though we were designed to be dependent on God and interdependent with others. Surrender requires that we admit dependence.

Danny's surrender to God's trustworthy love allowed optimism up close to death, which he practiced every day. Many people don't know that optimism is a possibility when death is close; imminent death brings only pessimism and despair. But Danny not only taught me that optimism is vital when we're facing death, he also helped me learn how that to achieve it I needed to surrender to God. He did this by asking a simple question.

One night at the hospital, Danny asked me, "What's the one thing that if you lost it would make life less worth living?"

Wow!

As a physically healthy twenty-two-year-old whose main concern was planning for the next weekend, I hadn't thought much about what might make life less worth living. Why would I? My life stretched out in front of me beyond my horizon. I could be carefree and live life with little care or intention.

Danny's question assumed that life was worth living. He was proving that by waking up each morning and getting into the day, every day. Because he had strung so many of these days together, we can easily miss this point, but Danny didn't. He was intentional about every day and savored each morning, afternoon, and evening. He embraced opportunities to make progress toward goals.

Danny's dependence on a loving, trustworthy God allowed him to fall asleep each night with the expectation that the next day would be better in spite of his circumstances. Danny showed me what it would be like to trust God. Although I was too early in my faith journey to fully accept his example, Danny's lesson eventually took hold in my life.

In many ways, a fatally ill fourteen-year-old was my most profound life-lesson teacher. Danny taught me to trust God and live with goal-oriented intention, which I now understand is a powerful combination that harnesses major brain circuits and resources.

Danny's question, "What's the one thing that if you lost it would make life less worth living?" has a corollary: "What's one thing that would make life more worth living?" I have asked this question in various ways to several thousand clients. It's the core of the Goaling Process[415] that I have taught in hundreds of medical schools and hospitals. It's the question I use with myself on a daily basis to help me be more intentional about how I live.

We all need to be linked to a valued future by meaningful goals we can share with others. We start by carefully developing healthy, well-rounded goals that describe the future we value. Once we identify those goals, we can be intentional in their pursuit. Danny knew he needed to be intentional and focused about how he spent his time. It was not acceptable to Danny for other people to set goals for him; he just didn't (literally) have the time.

Once Danny set a goal, he didn't put it on the shelf. He started planning and talking about it with others. As he talked about it, the path to the goal would become clearer and the goal would gather momentum.

The power of goals lies in their ability to focus how we spend our time and in encouraging others to join us in living life to the full. Joy! For Danny and me, his question set the stage for choosing whatever each of us identified as a goal that we would pursue; something to seek that would make life more worth living.

As it turned out, Danny did survive his time in the hospital and returned home. Was his goal to kiss Jane Fonda crucial? I don't know, but our support of this goal and many others helped him to understand that returning home was a possibility.

And Danny got that kiss. On the way to promoting new legislation for universal access to buildings for persons with disabilities, Danny was befriended by Jane and Henry Fonda, Nancy Sinatra, Joey Bishop, Bob Hope, and many others. Chuck Connors, television's "Rifleman," was my favorite Hollywood star because he actively cared for Danny and several other severely disabled children, making himself readily available for fundraising and other uplifting events.

But Danny's influence didn't stop with Hollywood; he was befriended also by the astronauts who visited the moon. While he was in our hospital, he entrusted me with moon rocks, a letter postmarked on the moon, and other memorabilia that were given to him because he had inspired them. How does anyone inspire a moon-walking astronaut? Is that possible? They're heroes to millions! Have you ever wondered who might be an astronaut's hero?

Danny gained famous friends and kisses and autographed photos and moon rocks because he inspired all of us to get beyond ourselves and live life to the full in spite of our circumstances. We were joyful in his presence.

My experience with Danny and many people since is that joyful goals shared with others pull us into valued futures. The power of joyful goals lies in their ability to focus how we spend our time living life to the full. As we push through obstacles that might seem overwhelming, joyful goals develop momentum. Often, I have to get out of my clients' way as they storm into their valued futures!

As things turn out when one is living intentionally, Danny achieved many of his goals and developed a purpose that changed the lives of many before he died in his sleep on December 27, 1970, at age fifteen. I had talked with him by phone on Christmas day; my last memory of Danny was his joyful voice. I don't remember what we discussed, but I know I was inspired by his presence in my life.

Since Danny's death, I have struggled with God, who has been very patient with me. For many years, I continued to live life on my own until I couldn't anymore, which is a story for another time. What I can share with you now is that Danny's example helped prepare me to handle the crisis that eventually came. Because I had known Danny, I realized my circumstances didn't dictate my joy and that God offered much more. When I hit bottom, I found many loving people waiting for me, most of them Jesus followers. I also found the Bible, which I now use as my primary reference. An ancient book that many people embrace and revere and others reject or despise, the Bible helps me fit in to God's created reality.

How Did the Bible Help You?

The Bible provides examples of the redemption of willful and broken people just like me. Given that the apostle Paul hit a hard bottom and experienced profound redemption and neurorehabilitation, I often look to his letters for pastoral guidance. Paul anticipated neuroscience. In addition to his apparent awareness of what we now call neuroplasticity, Paul taught about the need for intentional participation in adopting the character of Jesus and thereby developing our faithful brains. In his letter to the church in Colossae, Paul wrote,

> Put on then, as God's chosen ones, holy and beloved, compassion, kindness, lowliness, meekness, and patience, forbearing one another and, if one has a complaint against another, forgiving each other; as the Lord has forgiven you, so you also must forgive. And above all these put on love, which binds everything together in perfect harmony. (Colossians 3:12–14)

In this and many other lessons, Paul encouraged us to "put on" the character of Jesus, an active process requiring intention. Biblical scholar N. T. Wright pointed out that we need to participate in the development of our faithful brain because

> "each individual Christian must make the key choices to "put on" the things which genuinely anticipate, in the present, the life we are promised in the future, life we have already been given in Christ. And, having made those key choices, each Christian must acquire the habit of making them over and over again ... to create patterns of memory and imagination deep within the psyche, and as we saw from contemporary neuroscience, deep within the actual physical structure of our mysterious brain". [416] page 142

The path leading to the kingdom of heaven begins with redemption as we surrender to God. As we seek God's "good, pleasing and perfect will" for our lives, we begin brain transformation. This creates serenity in the brain, "the peace that passes all understanding" (Philippians 4:7).

We were created in the image of God, but we all have fallen short and tend to see ourselves out of focus and often darkly. As our faithful brain synchronizes with God, we come fully to life. As Paul explained, "For now we see only a reflection as in a mirror; then we shall see face to face. Now I know in part; then I shall know fully, even as I am fully known" (1 Corinthians 13:2).

Serenity is the condition of the brain when we are fully alive, trusting and relaxing in the embrace of God. The *Big Book* of Alcoholics Anonymous[417] promises, "we will comprehend the word serenity and we will know peace" as we abandon our old selves and surrender to God.

Figure 10 is my personal reminder of the brain's designed-in potential. I expect there is a picture of you somewhere that can be your personal reminder. Every child has the capacity for joy as the brain develops faithful to its design. When I am able to abandon my old self and surrender to God, serenity returns to my brain and releases the ecstatic joy of childhood. I gradually and more frequently realize this potential by allowing God to guide my faithful brain development. You can join me. Thank you for your time and attention.

Chapter Takeaways

1. Seeking God's will harnesses neuroplasticity to develop our faithful brain.
2. We begin to develop a faithful brain by adopting the character of Jesus.

3. Prayer, Bible study, and participating in communities of faith help develop a faithful brain.
4. Surrender to God leads to serenity in the brain, and joy is its predominant feeling.
5. Learning about brain structure and function complements our spiritual development.

Discussion Questions

1. What does Danny's story teach you about quality-of-life?
2. How can we experience joy regardless of our circumstances?
3. How does setting goals help us move forward into a valued future?
4. What is one thing you can do today to further adopt Jesus' character?

Glossary of Key Terms

Acetylcholine—One of many neurotransmitters in the autonomic nervous system. It controls skeletal and smooth muscles. Although it inhibits heart muscle and lowers heart rate, it excites nerve transmission and speeds up the musculoskeletal system. It's important for wakefulness, attentiveness, anger, aggression, and sexuality.

Amygdala—A brain structure that's part of the limbic system, the amygdala is located beneath each temporal lobe. The amygdala triggers our fight, flight, or freeze response and helps in the processing of memory, decision making, and emotional reactions. The amygdala is closely involved with the episodic autobiographical memory (EAM) network responsible for encoding, storage, and retrieval of these types of memories.

Anterior Cingulate Cortex—The front part of the cingulate cortex that resembles a "collar" surrounding the corpus callosum. The ACC helps to regulate blood pressure and heart rate. It also helps process emotions such as empathy. It's involved with the detection of errors, necessary for learning and problem solving. Anticipation of rewards occurs in the ACC, part of our decision making and impulse control.

Autonomic Nervous System—Beginning in the medulla oblongata in the lower brain stem and the tenth cranial nerve, the ANS is part of the peripheral nervous system. The ANS automatically functions below the level of consciousness to control functions such as breathing and heart rate, salivation and digestion, perspiration, and eye-pupil dilation. The ANS's three divisions are the sympathetic nervous system (SNS), the parasympathetic nervous system (PNS), and the enteric nervous system (ENS). The SNS is responsible for supporting our fight, flight, or freeze response. The PNS calms down the SNS. The ENS manages the gastrointestinal system.

Axon—The long, slender projection of a neuron that conducts electrical impulses away from the neuron's cell body to signal other neurons, muscles, and glands. It can be bare or covered with myelin, which insulates the axon and speeds up signal transmission. Because myelin is white, axons are described as the brain's "white matter."

Catecholamines—The fight, flight, or freeze hormones, dopamine, epinephrine (adrenaline), and norepinephrine (noradrenaline) that are released in response to stress. Several stimulant drugs mimic catecholamines or stimulate their production and release.

Cerebellum—A complex brain structure below the cerebrum, at the top of the brain stem. The covering of the cerebellum is a tightly packed sheet of neurons methodically arranged and integrated to provide smooth motor coordination. The cerebellum is also important for skilled motor learning that requires coordination of sensory input. Recently, the cerebellum has been identified as important for attention and language and in regulating fear and pleasure.

Cerebral Cortex—The outer cover of the cerebrum, also known as the "gray matter" that consists of neurons controlling many of our cognitive processes. Split into halves connected by the corpus callosum, the right and left hemispheres are not exactly the same size, and they perform different functions. The neocortex is the largest part of the cortex, consisting of up to six horizontal layers, each with a different composition of neurons and connections among neurons. The neocortex is approximately three millimeters thick, equivalent to six playing cards, with each layer having different functions and patterns of connections.

Cerebrum—Sitting at the top of the central nervous system, the cerebrum accounts for two-thirds of the brain's mass and is divided into two hemispheres linked by the corpus callosum. The cerebrum comprises the cerebral cortex as well as several sub-cortical structures, including the hippocampus, basal ganglia, and olfactory bulb. Each hemisphere has four lobes that control most of our cognitive and volitional function.

Cingulate Cortex—The cingulate cortex is situated in each hemisphere in the middle of and underneath the cerebral cortex. It's an integral part of the limbic system, which is involved with emotion formation and processing, learning, and memory. It provides the emotional salience to cognitive processes and is where thought is translated into emotion, including responses such as pain and terror.

Corpus Callosum—The corpus callosum is a fibrous bundle of approximately 250 million axons that connects the hemispheres of the cerebrum, allowing communication between the two.

Dendrite—The dendrite projects from a neuron cell body to receive and conduct the electrochemical or electrical signal from other neural cells to the cell body.

Dentate Gyrus—The dentate gyrus is a region in the human hippocampus that's involved with memory and learning. It's one of two brain structures currently known to produce neurogenesis in adults, with approximately 1,400 new neurons growing from stem cells in the dentate gyrus each day.

Dopamine—Dopamine is both a hormone and a neurotransmitter that's necessary for motivation, voluntary movement, lactation, sexual gratification, nausea, and attentiveness. Produced in the substantia nigra and the ventral tegmental area of the brain's reward network, its effect is increased by drugs such as cocaine and methamphetamine that increase seeking but not pleasure. Dopamine is important for addiction because of its effect on seeking behavior, in contrast to opiate drugs such as heroin or morphine that increase pleasure but don't alter seeking.

Endorphin—This is the contraction of the term *endogenous morphine*, meaning morphine that's produced in the body. More than twenty types of endorphins act as both hormones and neurotransmitters. Generally, their effect is to reduce pain and increase pleasure. Endorphins can be increased by exercise, ingesting foods such as chocolate and chili peppers, float tank relaxation, acupuncture, and breast feeding. Endorphins begin production in the placenta during the third month of pregnancy and affect both mother and child. Breast-feeding-induced endorphins may help avoid or minimize postpartum depression. Beta-endorphin is eighty times more potent an analgesic than morphine, produces relaxation and feelings of well-being, and may slow the growth of cancer cells.

Entorhinal Cortex—The entorhinal cortex (EC) is the main interface between the hippocampus and neocortex and so becomes the primary gateway for information sent to the hippocampus. It appears to pre-process the input signals in terms of familiarity based on information already received. The EC plays an important role in memory consolidation during sleep. The EC is one of the first areas to be affected by Alzheimer's disease, usually evidenced by an impaired sense of direction.

Epinephrine/Adrenaline—This chemical has two English names; it is both a hormone and a neurotransmitter that maintains alertness and blood pressure and is necessary for dealing with emergencies. Produced by the adrenal glands, in an emergency it makes glucose and oxygen available to the brain and large muscle groups, shunting blood from the gastrointestinal system.

Frontal Lobe—One of four of the cerebrum's lobes, the frontal lobe sits behind the forehead above the eyes and is the center of the cerebral cortex's executive function, especially with planning, organization, judgment, and self-control. This is the last part of the brain to develop and become fully connected, with completion in early adulthood.

Fusiform Face Area—The FFA is dedicated to identifying faces and making fine visual distinctions of well-known objects. It's near the fusiform gyrus, low on the temporal lobe where it meets the occipital lobe, which processes visual information. The FFA is also helpful for processing color information and symbols.

GABA—The acronym GABA stands for gamma-aminobutyric acid. GABA is a major inhibitory neurotransmitter. It helps to regulate anxiety and muscle tone. GABA is necessary for the growth of embryonic and neural stem cells and neurogenesis.

Glial Cells—The glial cells support neuron health, growth, and function. In the brain, glial cells are about ten times more numerous than neurons, but they vary in proportion across different nervous system regions. Glial cells guide brain development, maintain homeostasis, and provide housekeeping and protection for the neurons.

Glutamate—An excitatory neurotransmitter, glutamate is important for learning and memory. It's the most abundant excitatory neurotransmitter. Stored in vesicles at the synaptic cleft, nerve impulses trigger release of glutamate across the cleft to the postsynaptic cell, crucial for synaptic plasticity, also known as learning.

Happy Hippocampus Exercise—Similar to the Three Blessings Exercise developed at the University of Pennsylvania, this is a positive psychology intervention that takes advantage of the limited transfer of information from the hippocampus into long-term memories. Before dropping off to sleep, the individual recalls three episodes from the day in which he or she displayed more of an identified character trait than the day before. These episodes are among the last information entering the hippocampus before sleep, theoretically allowing greater opportunity for neuroconsolidation and integration into long-term memories.

Hippocampal Rehearsal—HR is an automatic process that's constantly recreating and reinforcing memories, orchestrated by the hippocampus and also involving the amygdala and cerebral cortex. The HR process is initiated every time a memory is recalled, recreating the memory. The recreated memory is influenced by the context in which HR occurs. Depending on the context and perspective of the person at that time, the recreated memory can be more or less accurate. Psychotherapy uses various methods to harness HR to create memories that facilitate emotional health.

Hippocampus—The hippocampus is under the cerebral cortex in the medial temporal lobe, next to the amygdala and extending rearward. Humans and other mammals have two hippocampi, one in each side of the brain. The hippocampus plays important roles in the consolidation of information from short-term memory to long-term memory and in spatial navigation. Most of the information that enters the hippocampus is discarded, while much of what remains is the source of "autobiographical memory."

Hypothalamus—The hypothalamus is a small portion of the brain below the thalamus, just above the brain stem. It's roughly the size of an almond and contains several small nuclei controlling many powerful functions. The hypothalamus links the nervous system to the endocrine system via the pituitary gland. It synthesizes and secretes releasing hormones that stimulate or inhibit the secretion of pituitary hormones. The hypothalamus monitors and regulates body status including temperature, thirst, hunger, and blood pressure and other activities of the autonomic nervous system. It also controls important aspects of parenting and attachment, fatigue, sleep, and circadian rhythm.

Insular Cortex—Part of the cerebral cortex structure, the IC is found in the lateral fissure between the temporal lobe and the frontal lobe. The IC controls autonomic functions through the regulation of the sympathetic and parasympathetic systems and is involved with self-awareness. The insular cortex is important for self-awareness, including motor control of the body in space and the body's internal states, emotional awareness, emotional salience, attention, addiction, and logical speech.

Limbic System—A complex set of brain structures, the limbic system lies on both sides of the thalamus, right under the cerebrum. The limbic system is composed of the hypothalamus, hippocampus, amygdala, and other structures that link the brain stem with the cerebral cortex. The limbic system is involved with motivation, emotion, learning and memory, initiating and controlling the emotions, instinctive behaviors, and the sense of smell.

Locus Ceruleus—The LC is a bluish segment of the brain stem involved with physiological responses to stress and panic. It's the brain's main source of norepinephrine.

Its norepinephrine has an excitatory effect on most of the brain, mediating arousal and priming neurons to be activated by stimuli. It's crucial in responding to new or surprising stimulation, and its dysfunction is implicated in depression, panic disorder, and anxiety. It influences neuroplasticity, arousal and the sleep-wake cycle, attention and memory, emotional tone, and behavioral flexibility as well as emotional inhibition and response to psychological stress.

Melatonin—Produced and secreted by the pineal gland in response to darkness, melatonin is an endocrine hormone that has many beneficial effects, including helping to bring about sleep. Its release is controlled by signals from the suprachiasmatic nucleus, next to the optic nerve that's entrained by the circadian rhythm of daylight and darkness. Melatonin functions to synchronize the biological clocks of many brain and body systems to bring about sleep. As children become teenagers, the nightly schedule of melatonin release is delayed, leading to later sleeping and waking times. In older adults, the pineal gland diminishes production of melatonin, leading to sleep problems in the elderly.

Mirror Neuron—A type of neuron implicated in imitation that may be necessary for empathy. Approximately 10 percent of human neurons may be of this type. It's involved in heated discussions about autism, theory of mind, and how to observe and interpret intentionality.

Neuroconsolidation—The organization of experiences into long-term memories. The ongoing process of creating long-term memories as information temporarily stored in the hippocampus is integrated into or extends existing neural networks and/or creates new neural networks. This is automatic, values-based neuroplasticity that brings personal truth to awareness, consciously experienced as Ah ha!

moments. Neuroconsolidation can be facilitated by brain-restorative sleep and guided by activities such as the Happy Hippocampus Exercise.

Neuron—A nerve cell. Adults have approximately 100 billion neurons with between 10 quadrillion and 100 quadrillion connections, participating in an uncountable number of neural networks and patterns. Neurons make up about 10 percent of brain mass, with much of the remaining mass attributable to glial cells.

Neuroplasticity—The constant pruning and linking of neurons with other neurons. Branching of dendrites and axons among neurons is guided by experience, the most efficacious of which have emotional salience. Neurons link with some neurons and are pruned from other neurons, reflecting learning and the individual's ongoing experience. Neuronal linkages are pruned or strengthened by the individual's thoughts, emotions, and experiences.

Norepinephrine/Noradrenaline—This chemical has two different English names. Norepinephrine is a precursor to epinephrine with similar action. It's a catecholamine that's both a hormone and a neurotransmitter released in response to stress and stimulation, directly increasing heart rate and the release of glucose. Norepinephrine is produced in the adrenal medulla and the locus ceruleus in response to new or abrupt stimulation. It's over-reactive in anxiety and in panic disorder and is under-reactive in depression.

Nucleus Accumbens—Located in the limbic system, the nucleus accumbens (NAc) is part of the brain's reward system. This is where information related to anticipation, reward, and motivation is processed. Most drugs that are abused and addicting act on the nucleus accumbens.

Occipital Lobe—The posterior segment of the cerebral cortex, the occipital lobe processes visual information and routes data regarding visual images to other parts of the brain for identification, naming, and storage.

Orbitofrontal Cortex—The orbitofrontal cortex (OFC) is a prefrontal region in the frontal lobes involved in the cognitive processing of decision making. This is part of the frontal cortex above the orbits of the eyes that is involved in judgment, discernment, wisdom, and other cognitive processes.

Oxytocin—A neuropeptide produced in the hypothalamus that is released by the pituitary gland in large amounts during labor and in smaller amounts during breast feeding. Oxytocin is a hormone and neurotransmitter. Oxytocin flows in the bodies of infants, strongly stimulated by maternal love and simulated at a lower level by paternal love. Oxytocin flows in the bodies of adults, stimulated by trustworthy love. It stimulates parental behavior, sacrificial love, trust, and generosity. It also helps to inhibit the amygdala, which is the key brain structure that triggers the fear response, and it can indirectly inhibit the release of cortisol, an important stress hormone.

Parietal Lobe—The parietal lobe is the segment of the cerebral cortex above the temporal lobe and between the occipital lobe and the frontal lobe. The parietal lobe receives and processes information from the body and integrates sensory information among various modalities, including spatial sense and navigation. The parietal lobe is implicated in calculating the location and speed of objects.

Serotonin—Serotonin is a neurotransmitter that helps regulate appetite, body temperature, sleep, mood, emotion, and memory. Serotonin has strong associations with depression in that it appears to signal an impoverished environment. Serotonin levels are affected by diet, because it's made from tryptophan, which is available only through food. Dates, papayas, bananas, oats, milk, and yogurt are good sources of tryptophan.

Suprachiasmatic Nucleus—The suprachiasmatic nucleus (SCN) is a tiny group of neurons directly above the optic chiasm in the hypothalamus that are responsible for maintaining circadian rhythm. The SCN is pine cone–shaped and the size of a grain of rice. It contains several cell types and different peptides, including vasopressin and neurotransmitters. The SCN sends information to the hypothalamus and the pineal gland to modulate body temperature and release hormones such as cortisol and melatonin.

Synapse—The gap between neurons that chemical signals or electrical signals span to trigger or inhibit nerve cell electrical signals that propagate down the axon of one cell to the dendrites of another.

Temporal Lobe—The temporal lobe, one of the four major lobes of the cerebral cortex, is beneath the lateral fissure on both cerebral hemispheres of the brain. The temporal lobes are involved in the retention of visual memories, processing sensory input, comprehending language, storing new memories, emotion, and deriving meaning. For most people, the left temporal lobe is the center of language reception, processing, and production.

Temporoparietal Junction—The temporoparietal junction (TPJ) sits between the temporal lobe and the parietal lobe and is activated when we consider other people's intentions and thoughts. The TPJ plays a crucial role in self-other distinction processes and theory of mind. Damage to the TPJ diminishes the ability to make moral decisions.

Thalamus—Located on the top of the brain stem, the thalamus acts as a relay station that sorts and processes signals to and from the spinal cord and brain structures up to the cerebrum and down to the nervous system.

Ventral Tegmental Area—The ventral tegmental area (VTA) is in the midbrain between several other major areas, reciprocally connected with many structures throughout the brain. The nucleus accumbens (NAc) and the ventral tegmental area (VTA) are the primary activation sites for drugs of abuse including heroin, cocaine, alcohol, opiates, marijuana, nicotine, and amphetamine. These drugs prolong the action of dopamine in the nucleus accumbens or potentiate the activation of neurons in the VTA and NAc. The most common drugs of abuse stimulate the release of dopamine, which creates both rewarding and psychomotor effects.

Ventromedial Prefrontal Cortex—The ventromedial prefrontal cortex (VMPFC) is in the frontal lobe at the bottom of the cerebral hemispheres. Crucial for decision making in uncertainty, the VMPFC is also involved in the processing of future consequences, balancing risks and rewards, and developing appropriate responses to fear. It's involved in moderating emotions and emotional reactions and in processing gender-specific social cues. This is the last area of the cerebral cortex to develop.

Acknowledgments

This book is the result of the efforts of several people I want to acknowledge, each of whom has enriched my life.

My wife and family have been very patient with me for the last seven years. Kristen, Jonathan, Max, and Erin have created space and time for me to move this project forward and have encouraged me at every turn. My wife, Mary Marland Matheson, has read and re-read the manuscripts and offered constructive criticism. Telling me "No, it's not ready" several times, Mary has encouraged me to keep with it for several years. Her patience and dedication to me and this project inspire me and are greatly appreciated.

For the first year of the project, I met weekly with Russ Kirkland and Dale Tiemann. Taking our cue from the *Inklings* of C. S. Lewis, J.R.R. Tolkien, and their friends, we read each other's work, shared ideas, and fanned the flame. It caught fire and has burned steadily since.

Over the past four years, Mark Dungan and Tony Ruesing have steadfastly participated in our joint exploration of faith and neuroscience. We meet weekly to discuss these issues and explore difficult questions. Mark and Tony have read several versions of this manuscript, leading to important changes. Mark has been an amazing developmental editor, graciously offering hundreds of hours to read, question, comment, and encourage. Mark's wife, Judy Dungan, is very good at asking insightful questions and won't settle for uninformed answers, which has helped me to grow.

My good friend Bryan Kemp is another person who asks many good questions and won't settle for easy answers. Dr. Kemp is the foremost expert on how the psychology of disability affects quality of life, scientifically demonstrating that it's our purpose in life rather than our circumstances that determine our ability to live life to the full. His example inspires me and his encouragement is deeply valued.

In the past year, Bible scholar Matt Lybarger joined our project, providing valuable theological support. Matt is an associate pastor at The Crossing who has helped me understand how and for whom the Bible was written, which has deepened its meaning and broadened my appreciation of Jesus.

Patti Kirkland has joined Mary in encouraging better examples and case studies to elucidate potentially difficult neuroscientific issues. I have fond memories of discussions of faith and neuroscience with Patti, her husband, Russ, and Mary while traveling together.

Over the past five years, I have taken the opportunity to share with my graduate students and colleagues at Covenant Theological Seminary various segments of this book. Their questions have helped me understand what needs to be explained better. Learning to explain difficult ideas has been an important part of my growth, for which I will always be grateful.

Finally, I want to acknowledge my clients. Beginning with Danny Munday on the first day of my career on February 3, 1970, my life has been deeply enriched by their lives. Their trust and openness have been the basis of my growth as a person and as a professional. I hope I have represented you well.

References

1. Baker, J. *NIV Celebrate Recovery Bible*. 2007. Grand Rapids, MI: Zondervan.
2. Kandel, E. et al. eds. *Principles of Neural Science*. 5th ed. 2013. New York: McGraw Hill Medical, 1709.
3. Willard, D. *Renovation of the Heart: Putting on the Character of Christ*. 2012. Colorado Springs, CO: NavPress.
4. Schmitz, C. and P. Hof. *Design-based stereology in neuroscience*. Neuroscience, 2005. **130**(4): 813–31.
5. Abitz, M. et al. *Excess of neurons in the human newborn mediodorsal thalamus compared with that of the adult*. Cerebral Cortex, 2007. **17**(11): 2573–78.
6. Herculano-Houzel, S. *The human brain in numbers: a linearly scaled-up primate brain*. Frontiers in human neuroscience, 2009. **3**.
7. Herculano-Houzel, S. *The remarkable, yet not extraordinary, human brain as a scaled-up primate brain and its associated cost*. Proc Natl Acad Sci U S A. 2012. **109 Suppl 1**: 10661–68.
8. Lezak, M., D. Howieson, and D. Loring. *Neuropsychological Assessment*. 4th ed. 2004. Oxford: Oxford University Press. 1016.
9. Frith, C. *Disorders of Conscious and Unconscious Mental Processes*, in *Principles of Neural Science*, E. Kandel et al. eds. 2013. New York: McGraw Hill Medical: 1373–88.

10. Baudrexel, S. et al. *Resting state fMRI reveals increased subthalamic nucleus–motor cortex connectivity in Parkinson's disease.* Neuroimage. 2011. **55**(4): 1728–38.
11. Schonberg, T. et al. *Selective impairment of prediction error signaling in human dorsolateral but not ventral striatum in Parkinson's disease patients: evidence from a model-based fMRI study.* Neuroimage. 2010. **49**(1): 772–81.
12. Cerasa, A. et al. *Prefrontal alterations in Parkinson's disease with levodopa-induced dyskinesia during fMRI motor task.* Movement Disorders, 2012. **27**(3): 364–71.
13. Kahan, J. et al. *Resting state functional MRI in Parkinson's disease: the impact of deep brain stimulation on 'effective' connectivity.* Brain. 2014: awu027.
14. Koch, C. *The Neuroscience of Consciousness*, in *Fundamental Neuroscience*, L. Squire et al. editors. 2013. Waltham, MA: Academic Press, 1091–1103.
15. Kriegeskorte, N., R. Cusack, and P. Bandettini. *How does an fMRI voxel sample the neuronal activity pattern: compact-kernel or complex spatiotemporal filter?* Neuroimage. 2010. **49**(3): 1965–76.
16. Fox, M. D. et al. *The human brain is intrinsically organized into dynamic, anticorrelated functional networks.* Proc Natl Acad Sci U S A. 2005. **102**(27): 9673–78.
17. Kragel, P. A., R. M. Carter, and S. A. Huettel. *What makes a pattern? Matching decoding methods to data in multivariate pattern analysis.* Front Neurosci, 2012. **6**: 162.
18. Seung, S. *Connectome: How the brain's wiring makes us who we are.* 2012. New York: Houghton Mifflin Harcourt.
19. Hawkins, J. and S. Blakeslee. *On intelligence.* 1st ed. 2004. New York: Times Books, 261.

20. Damasio, A. R. *Descartes' Error: Emotion, Reason, and the Human Brain.* 1994. London: Penguin Books.
21. Kandel, E. *From Nerve Cells to Cognition: The internal representation of thought and action,* in *Principles of Neural Science,* E. Kandel et al. eds. 2013. New York: McGraw Hill Medical: 370–91.
22. Hebb, D. O. *The organization of behavior: A neuropsychological theory.* 1949. New York: John Wiley & Sons.
23. Miyawaki, Y. et al. *Visual image reconstruction from human brain activity using a combination of multiscale local image decoders.* Neuron, 2008. **60**(5): 915–29.
24. Jarrell, T. A. et al. *The connectome of a decision-making neural network.* Science, 2012. **337**(6093): 437–44.
25. Barch, D. M. et al. *Function in the human connectome: Task-fMRI and individual differences in behavior.* NeuroImage, 2013. **80**(0): 169–89.
26. Koyama, M. S. et al. *Cortical signatures of dyslexia and remediation: an intrinsic functional connectivity approach.* PLoS One, 2013. **8**(2): e55454.
27. Van Essen, D. C. et al. *The WU-Minn Human Connectome Project: An overview.* Neuroimage, 2013.
28. Doidge, N. *The brain that changes itself: Stories of personal triumph from the frontiers of brain science.* 2007. New York: Viking. xvi, 427.
29. Dayan, E. and L. G. Cohen. *Neuroplasticity subserving motor skill learning.* Neuron. 2011. **72**(3): 443–54.
30. Draganski, B. et al. *Neuroplasticity: changes in grey matter induced by training.* Nature. 2004. **427**(6972): 311–12.
31. Jung, R. E. et al. *The structure of creative cognition in the human brain.* Front Hum Neurosci, 2013. **7**: 330.

32. Pittenger, C. and R. S. Duman. *Stress, depression, and neuroplasticity: a convergence of mechanisms.* Neuropsychopharmacology, 2008. **33**(1):88–109.
33. Jessell, T. and J. Sanes. *Differentiation and Survival of Nerve Cells*, in *Principles of Neural Science*, E. Kandel et al. eds. 2013. New York: McGraw Hill Medical: 1187–1208.
34. Hosoda, C. et al. *Dynamic neural network reorganization associated with second langauage vocabulary acquisition: A multimodal imaging study.* The Journal of Neuroscience, 2013. **33**(34): 13663–672.
35. Struthers, W. M. *Wired for intimacy: How pornography hijacks the male brain.* 2009. Downers Grove, IL: InterVarsity Press.
36. Tanaka, S. et al. *Larger right posterior parietal volume in action video game experts: A behavioral and voxel-based morphometry (VBM) study.* PLoS One, 2013. **8**(6): e66998.
37. Münte, T. F., E. Altenmüller, and L. Jäncke. *The musician's brain as a model of neuroplasticity.* Nature Reviews Neuroscience, 2002. **3**(6):473–78.
38. Sanes, J. and T. Jessell. *Repairing the Damaged Brain*, in *Principles of Neural Science*, E. Kandel et al. eds. 2013. New York: McGraw Hill Medical: 1284–1305.
39. Harris, W. A., V. Hartenstein, and M. Goulding. *Cellular Determination*, in *Fundamental Neuroscience*, L. R. Squire et al. eds. 2013. New York: Academic Press: 1127.
40. Sanes, J. and T. Jessell. *The Aging Brain*, in *Principles of Neural Science*, E. Kandel et al. eds. 2013. New York: McGraw Hill Medical: 1328–46.
41. Hyman, S. and J. Cohen. *Disorders of Mood and Anxiety*, in *Principles of Neural Science*, E. Kandel et al. Editors. 2013, New York: McGraw Hill Medical, 1402–1424.

42. Eisch, A. J. and D. Petrik. *Depression and hippocampal neurogenesis: a road to remission?* Science, 2012. **338**(6103): 72.
43. Gottlieb, G. *Normally occurring environmental and behavioral influences on gene activity: From central dogma to probabilistic epigenesis.* Psychological Review, 1998. **105**(4):792–802.
44. Gottlieb, G. *Developmental-behavioral initiation of evolutionary change.* Psychological Review, 2002. **109**(2): 211–18.
45. Gottlieb, G. *Probabilistic epigenesis.* Developmental Science, 2007. **10**(1): 1–11.
46. Gapp, K. et al. *Early life epigenetic programming and transmission of stress-induced traits in mammals.* BioEssays, 2014.
47. Siegel, D. *The Developing Mind: How Relationships and the Brain Interact to Shape Who We Are.* 2nd Edition ed. 2012, New York: Guilford Press.
48. Keverne, E. B. *Significance of epigenetics for understanding brain development, brain evolution and behaviour.* Neuroscience. 2012.
49. Zhang, T. Y. et al. *Epigenetic mechanisms for the early environmental regulation of hippocampal glucocorticoid receptor gene expression in rodents and humans.* Neuropsychopharmacology, 2013. **38**(1): 111–23.
50. Saab, B. J. and I. M. Mansuy. *Neurobiological disease etiology and inheritance: an epigenetic perspective.* The Journal of Experimental Biology, 2014. **217**(1):94–101.
51. Roberts, A. L. et al. *Women's experience of abuse in childhood and their children's smoking and overweight.* American Journal of Preventive Medicine, 2014. **46**(3): 249–58.

52. Lehrner, A. et al. *Maternal PTSD associates with greater glucocorticoid sensitivity in offspring of Holocaust survivors.* Psychoneuroendocrinology, 2014. **40**: 213–20.
53. Van den Berg, G. J. and P. Pinger. *A validation study of transgenerational effects of childhood conditions on the third generation offspring's economic and health outcomes potentially driven by epigenetic imprinting.* 2014. Bonn, Germany: Institute for the Study of Labor.
54. Pitman, R. K. et al. *Biological studies of post-traumatic stress disorder.* Nat Rev Neurosci, 2012. **13**(11): 769–87.
55. Gräff, J. et al. *Epigenetic priming of memory updating during reconsolidation to attenuate remote fear memories.* Cell, 2014. **156**(1): 261–76.
56. Siegelbaum, S. and E. Kandel. *Prefrontal Cortex, Hippocampus, and the Biology of Explicit Memory Storage*, in *Principles of Neural Science*. Kandel, E. et al., eds. 2013. New York: McGraw Hill Medical. 1487–1521.
57. Canli, T. and K.-P. Lesch. *Long story short: The serotonin transporter in emotion regulation and social cognition.* Nature Neuroscience, 2007. **10**(9):1103-09.
58. Mueller, A. et al. *Interaction of serotonin transporter gene-linked polymorphic region and stressful life events predicts cortisol stress response.* Neuropsychopharmacology. 2011. **36**(7):1332–39.
59. Lesch, K. P. *Linking emotion to the social brain.* EMBO reports, 2007. **8**(1S):S24–S29.
60. Kamitani, Y. and F. Tong. *Decoding the visual and subjective contents of the human brain.* Nat Neurosci, 2005. **8**(5):679–85.
61. Rabinovich, M., I. Tristan, and P. Varona. *Neural dynamics of attentional cross-modality control.* PLoS One, 2013. **8**(5):e64406.

62. Sui, J., P. Rotshtein, and G. W. Humphreys. *Coupling social attention to the self forms a network for personal significance.* Proc Natl Acad Sci U S A, 2013. **110**(19):7607–12.
63. Ainsworth, M. D. *Attachments beyond infancy.* Am Psychol, 1989. **44**(4):709–16.
64. Porges, S. *Love: An emergent property of the mammalian autonomic nervous system.* Psychoneuroendocrinology, 1998. **23**(8):837–61.
65. Henslin, E. R. and B. F. Johnson, *This is your brain in love: New scientific breakthroughs for a more passionate and emotionally healthy marriage.* 2009. Nashville, TN: Thomas Nelson. 212.
66. Gouin, J. P. et al. *Marital behavior, oxytocin, vasopressin, and wound healing.* Psychoneuroendocrinology, 2010. **35**(7):1082–90.
67. Esch, T. and G. B. Stefano. *The neurobiological link between compassion and love.* Med Sci Monit, 2011. **17**(3):RA65–75.
68. Saphire-Bernstein, S. et al. *Oxytocin receptor gene (OXTR) is related to psychological resources.* Proceedings of the National Academy of Sciences, 2011. **108**(37):15118–122.
69. Acevedo, B. P. et al. *Neural correlates of long-term intense romantic love.* Soc Cogn Affect Neurosci, 2012. **7**(2):145–59.
70. Feldman, R. *Oxytocin and social affiliation in humans.* Horm Behav, 2012. **61**(3):380–91.
71. Carter, C. S. and S. W. Porges. *The biochemistry of love: An oxytocin hypothesis.* EMBO Rep, 2013. **14**(1):12–16.
72. Bethlehem, R. A. et al. *Oxytocin, brain physiology, and functional connectivity: A review of intranasal oxytocin fMRI studies.* Psychoneuroendocrinology, 2013. **38**(7):962–74.

73. Arseneault, L. et al. *Childhood trauma and children's emerging psychotic symptoms: a genetically sensitive longitudinal cohort study.* American Journal of Psychiatry, 2011. **168**(1):65–72.
74. Fisher, H. L. et al. *Reliability and comparability of psychosis patients' retrospective reports of childhood abuse.* Schizophrenia bulletin, 2011. **37**(3):546–53.
75. De Bellis, M. D. *The neurobiology of child neglect*, in *The Impact of Early Life Trauma on Health and Disease: The hidden epidemic*, R. A. Lanius, E. Vermetten, and C. Pain, eds. 2010, Cambridge: Cambridge University Press. 123–32.
76. Belsky, J. and M. de Haan. *Annual research review: Parenting and children's brain development: The end of the beginning.* Journal of Child Psychology and Psychiatry, 2011. **52**(4):409–28.
77. Wilson, K. R., D. J. Hansen, and M. Li. *The traumatic stress response in child maltreatment and resultant neuropsychological effects.* Aggression and violent behavior, 2011. **16**(2):87–97.
78. Korosi, A. et al. *Early life experience reduces excitation to stress-responsive hypothalamic neurons and reprograms the expression of corticotropin-releasing hormone.* The Journal of Neuroscience, 2010. **30**(2):703–13.
79. Cozolino, L. *The Neuroscience of Human Relationships: Attachment And the Developing Social Brain.* 2006, New York: W. W. Norton.
80. Newberg, A. B. *The neuroscientific study of spiritual practices.* Frontiers in psychology, 2014. **5**.
81. Biswal, B. B. et al. *Toward discovery science of human brain function.* Proc Natl Acad Sci U S A, 2010. **107**(10):4734–39.

82. Kelly, C. et al. *Characterizing variation in the functional connectome: Promise and pitfalls.* Trends Cogn Sci, 2012. **16**(3):181–88.
83. Deisseroth, K. et al. *Next-generation optical technologies for illuminating genetically targeted brain circuits.* The Journal of Neuroscience, 2006. **26**(41):10380–386.
84. Arden, J. B. *Rewire your brain: Think your way to a better life.* 2010, Hoboken, NJ: John Wiley & Sons.
85. Arden, J. B. and L. Linford. *Brain-based therapy with children and adolescents: Evidence-based treatment for everyday practice.* 2008, Hoboken, NJ: John Wiley & Sons.
86. Arden, J. B. and L. Linford. *Brain-based therapy with adults: Evidence-based treatment for everyday practice.* 2008, Hoboken, NJ: John Wiley & Sons.
87. Moreland, J. P. and D. Willard. *Love your God with all your mind: The role of reason in the life of the soul.* 1997, Colorado Springs, CO: NavPress.
88. Jeeves, M. and W. Brown. *Neuroscience, psychology, and religion: Illusions, delusions, and realities about human nature.* 2009, West Conshohoken, PA: Templeton Foundation Press.
89. Porges, S. W. *The Polyvagal Theory: Neurophysiological Foundations of Emotions, Attachment, Communication, and Self-regulation.* 2011: W. W. Norton.
90. Porges, S. W. and S. A. Furman. *The early development of the autonomic nervous system provides a neural platform for social behaviour: A polyvagal perspective.* Infant and Child Development, 2011. **20**(1):106–18.
91. Cooper, D. C., J. F. Thayer, and S. R. Waldstein. *Coping with Racism: The impact of prayer on cardiovascular reactivity and post-stress recovery in African-American women.* Ann Behav Med, 2014. **47**(2):218–30.

92. Park, G. et al. *Cardiac vagal tone predicts attentional engagement to and disengagement from fearful faces.* Emotion, 2013. **13**(4):645–56.
93. Park, G. et al. *Cardiac vagal tone is correlated with selective attention to neutral distractors under load.* Psychophysiology, 2013. **50**(4):398–406.
94. Thayer, J. F. et al. *A meta-analysis of heart rate variability and neuroimaging studies: Implications for heart rate variability as a marker of stress and health.* Neuroscience & Biobehavioral Reviews, 2012. **36**(2):747–56.
95. Sperry, R. W. *A powerful paradigm made stronger.* Neuropsychologia, 1998. **36**(10):1063–68.
96. Sperry, R. W. *Mind-brain interaction: mentalism, yes; dualism, no.* Neuroscience, 1980. **5**(2):195–206.
97. Sperry, R. W. *A unifying approach to mind and brain: ten year perspective.* Prog Brain Res, 1976. **45**:463–69.
98. Sperry, R. W. *Hemisphere deconnection and unity in conscious awareness.* Am Psychol, 1968. **23**(10):723–33.
99. Sperry, R. W. *Cerebral Organization and Behavior: The split brain behaves in many respects like two separate brains, providing new research possibilities.* Science, 1961. **133**(3466):1749–57.
100. Gazzaniga, M. S. *Forty-five years of split-brain research and still going strong.* Nat Rev Neurosci, 2005. **6**(8):653-59.
101. Funk, C. M. and M. S. Gazzaniga. *The functional brain architecture of human morality.* Curr Opin Neurobiol, 2009. **19**(6):678–81.
102. Gazzaniga, M. S. *Neuroscience in the courtroom.* Sci Am, 2011. **304**(4):54–59.
103. Doron, K. W., D. S. Bassett, and M. S. Gazzaniga. *Dynamic network structure of interhemispheric coordination.* Proc Natl Acad Sci U S A, 2012. **109**(46):18661–668.

104. Aharoni, E. et al. *Neuroprediction of future rearrest.* Proc Natl Acad Sci U S A, 2013. **110**(15):6223–28.
105. Gazzaniga, M. S., *Shifting gears: seeking new approaches for mind/brain mechanisms.* Annu Rev Psychol, 2013. **64**:1–20.
106. Koenigs, M. et al. *Damage to the prefrontal cortex increases utilitarian moral judgements.* Nature, 2007. **446**(7138):908–11.
107. Preston, S. D. et al. *The neural substrates of cognitive empathy.* Soc Neurosci, 2007. **2**(3–4):254–75.
108. Immordino-Yang, M. H. et al. *Neural correlates of admiration and compassion.* Proc Natl Acad Sci USA, 2009. **106**(19):8021–26.
109. Young, L. et al. *Damage to ventromedial prefrontal cortex impairs judgment of harmful intent.* Neuron, 2010. **65**(6):845–51.
110. Philippi, C. L. et al. *Preserved self-awareness following extensive bilateral brain damage to the insula, anterior cingulate, and medial prefrontal cortices.* PLoS One, 2012. **7**(8):e38413.
111. Man, K. et al. *Neural convergence and divergence in the mammalian cerebral cortex: from experimental neuroanatomy to functional neuroimaging.* J Comp Neurol, 2013.
112. Siegel, D. *Memory: an overview, with emphasis on developmental, interpersonal, and neurobiological aspects.* J Am Acad Child Adolesc Psychiatry, 2001. **40**(9):997–1011.
113. Cozolino, L. *The Neuroscience of Psychotherapy: Healing the Social Brain.* 2nd ed. 2010, New York: W. W. Norton.
114. Badenoch, B. and P. Cox. *Integrating interpersonal neurobiology with group psychotherapy.* Int J Group Psychother, 2010. **60**(4):462–81.

115. Siegel, D. *The mindful therapist: A clinician's guide to mindsight and neural integration.* Norton Series on Interpersonal Neurobiology. 2010, New York: W. W. Norton.
116. Siegel, D. J. *The Mindful Brain: Reflection and Attunement in the Cultivation of Well-Being (Norton Series on Interpersonal Neurobiology).* 2007: W. W. Norton.
117. Grippo, A. J. et al. *Oxytocin protects against negative behavioral and autonomic consequences of long-term social isolation.* Psychoneuroendocrinology, 2009. **34**(10):1542–53.
118. Carter, C. S. et al. *Oxytocin, vasopressin and sociality.* Prog Brain Res, 2008. **170**:331–36.
119. Baumgartner, T. et al. *Oxytocin shapes the neural circuitry of trust and trust adaptation in humans.* Neuron, 2008. **58**(4):639–50.
120. Heinrichs, M. et al. *Social support and oxytocin interact to suppress cortisol and subjective responses to psychosocial stress.* Biological Psychiatry, 2003. **54**(12):1389–98.
121. Hurlemann, R. et al. *Oxytocin enhances amygdala-dependent, socially reinforced learning and emotional empathy in humans.* The Journal of Neuroscience, 2010. **30**(14):4999–5007.
122. Peterson, C. and M. Seligman. *Character strengths and virtues: A handbook and classification.* 2004, Oxford: Oxford University Press.
123. Thompson, C. *Anatomy of the Soul: Surprising Connections between Neuroscience and Spiritual Practices That Can Transform Your Life and Relationships.* 2010, Carol Stream, IL: Tyndale House.
124. Tangney, J. P. and D. J. Mashek. *In Search of the Moral Person,* in *Handbook of Experimental Existential Psychology,* J. Greenberg and S. L. Koole, eds. 2004. 160.

125. Debiec, J., J. E. LeDoux, and K. Nader. *Cellular and systems reconsolidation in the hippocampus.* Neuron, 2002. **36**(3):527–38.
126. Loftus, E. F. *Make-believe memories.* American Psychologist, 2003. **58**(11):867.
127. Battaglia, F. P. et al. *The hippocampus: Hub of brain network communication for memory.* Trends in Cognitive Sciences, 2011. **15**(7):310–18.
128. Amico, F. et al. *Structural MRI correlates for vulnerability and resilience to major depressive disorder.* Journal of psychiatry & neuroscience: JPN, 2011. **36**(1):15–22.
129. Frodl, T. and V. O'Keane. *How does the brain deal with cumulative stress? A review with focus on developmental stress, HPA axis function and hippocampal structure in humans.* Neurobiology of disease, 2013. **52**:24–37.
130. Frodl, T. et al. *Association of the brain-derived neurotrophic factor Val66Met polymorphism with reduced hippocampal volumes in major depression.* Archives of General Psychiatry, 2007. **64**(4):410–16.
131. Ellison, C. G. et al. *Prayer, attachment to God, and symptoms of anxiety-related disorders among US adults.* Sociology of Religion, 2014. **75**(2):208–33.
132. Yancey, P. *What's So Amazing About Grace?* 1997, Grand Rapids, MI: Zondervan.
133. Duhigg, C. *The power of habit: why we do what we do in life and business.* 2012: Random House.
134. Emmons, R. A. *Gratitude Works!: A 21-Day Program for Creating Emotional Prosperity.* 2013: John Wiley & Sons.
135. Emmons, R. A. and T. E. Kneezel. *Giving thanks: Spiritual and religious correlates of gratitude.* Journal of Psychology and Christianity, 2005. **24**(2):140.

136. Emmons, R. A. and R. Stern. *Gratitude as a psychotherapeutic intervention.* Journal of Clinical Psychology, 2013. **69**(8):846–55.
137. Jacobsen, E. *Progressive relaxation.* 1929, Oxford, England: Univ. of Chicago Press. 429.
138. Benson, H., J. Beary, and M. Carol. *The relaxation response.* Psychiatry: Journal for the Study of Interpersonal Processes, 1974. **37**(1):37–46.
139. Feldman, G., J. Greeson, and J. Senville. *Differential effects of mindful breathing, progressive muscle relaxation, and loving-kindness meditation on decentering and negative reactions to repetitive thoughts.* Behaviour Research and Therapy, 2010. **48**(10):1002–11.
140. Miller, W. R. *Integrating spirituality into treatment: Resources for practitioners.* 1999: American Psychological Association.
141. Emmons, R. A. *Thanks!: How the new science of gratitude can make you happier.* 2007: Houghton Mifflin Harcourt.
142. Seligman, M. E. et al. *Positive psychology progress: empirical validation of interventions.* American psychologist, 2005. **60**(5):410.
143. Park, N. and C. Peterson. *Characterizing Resilience and Growth Among Soldiers: A Trajectory Study*, 2012, DTIC Document.
144. Bandura, A. *Self-efficacy mechanism in psychobiologic functioning*, in *Self-Efficacy: Thought control of action*, R. Schwarzer, ed. 1992, New York: Taylor & Francis. 355–94.
145. Bandura, A. *Self-efficacy.* 1994: Wiley Online Library.
146. Farmer, R. F. and A. L. Chapman. *Behavioral Interventions in Cognitive Behavior Therapy.* 2008, Washington, DC: American Psychological Association.

147. American Psychiatric Association. *Diagnostic and statistical manual of mental disorders: DSM-5.* Fifth ed. 2013, Washington, DC: Amer Psychiatric Pub. 947.
148. Morina, N. et al. *Remission from post-traumatic stress disorder in adults: A systematic review and meta-analysis of long term outcome studies.* Clin Psychol Rev, 2014. **34**(3):249–55.
149. Bisson, J. I. et al. *Psychological therapies for chronic post-traumatic stress disorder (PTSD) in adults.* Cochrane Database Syst Rev, 2013. **12**:CD003388.
150. Santiago, P. N. et al. *A systematic review of PTSD prevalence and trajectories in DSM-5 defined trauma exposed populations: intentional and non-intentional traumatic events.* PLoS One, 2013. **8**(4):e59236.
151. Steenkamp, M. M., W. P. Nash, and B. T. Litz. *Post-Traumatic Stress Disorder: Review of the Comprehensive Soldier Fitness Program.* American Journal of Preventive Medicine, 2013. **44**(5):507–12.
152. Skeffington, P. M., C. S. Rees, and R. Kane. *The primary prevention of PTSD: A systematic review.* Journal of Trauma & Dissociation, 2013. **14**(4):404–22.
153. Cornum, R., M. D. Matthews, and M. E. Seligman. *Comprehensive soldier fitness: Building resilience in a challenging institutional context.* American Psychologist, 2011. **66**(1):4.
154. Griffith, J. and C. West. *Master resilience training and its relationship to individual well-being and stress buffering among Army National Guard soldiers.* The Journal of Behavioral Health Services & Research, 2013. **40**(2):140–55.
155. Damasio, A. *Neuroscience and ethics: Intersections.* Am Journal of Bioethics, 2007. **7**(1):3–7.

156. Kahneman, D. and A. Tversky. *Choices, values, and frames.* American Psychologist, 1984. **39**(4):341.
157. Kahneman, D. *A perspective on judgment and choice: mapping bounded rationality.* American Psychologist, 2003. **58**(9):697.
158. Kahneman, D. *Thinking, Fast and Slow.* 2011, New York: Farrar, Straus & Giroux.
159. Sharot, T. et al. *Neural mechanisms mediating optimism bias.* Nature, 2007. **450**(7166):102–05.
160. Cooper, J. C. and B. Knutson. *Valence and salience contribute to nucleus accumbens activation.* Neuroimage, 2008. **39**(1):538–47.
161. Borsook, D. et al. *Pain and Analgesia: The value of salience circuits.* Progress in Neurobiology, 2013. **104**(May):93–105.
162. Wang, L. et al. *ERP evidence on the interaction between information structure and emotional salience of words.* Cognitive, Affective, & Behavioral Neuroscience, 2013. **13**(2):297–310.
163. Levitin, D. J. *This is your brain on music: The science of a human obsession.* 2006.
164. Vines, B. W. et al. *Music to my eyes: Cross-modal interactions in the perception of emotions in musical performance.* Cognition, 2011. **118**(2):157–70.
165. Chanda, M. L. and D. J. Levitin. *The neurochemistry of music.* Trends in Cognitive Sciences, 2013. **17**(4):179–93.
166. cummings, e. *[i carry your heart with me(i carry it in].* Poetry, 1952.
167. Matheson, L. *i carry your heart with me (i carry it in my heart) by ee cummings.* [video] 2010; available from: http://youtu.be/Y1-nwU6TS4o.

168. Warren, R. *The purpose driven church: Growth without compromising your message & mission.* 1995, Grand Rapids, MI: Zondervan.
169. Scazzero, P. and W. Bird. *The Emotionally Healthy Church.* 2003, Grand Rapids, MI: Zondervan.
170. Lewis, C. S. *The Screwtape Letters.* 2011, New York: HarperCollins.
171. Rogers, C. R. *The characteristics of a helping relationship.* Personnel and Guidance Journal, 1958. **37**:6–16.
172. Rogers, C. R. *On becoming a person: A therapist's view of psychotherapy.* 1995, New York: Houghton Mifflin Harcourt.
173. Rogers, C. R. *Client-centered therapy: Its current practice, implications and theory.* 1951 Boston: Houghton Mifflin.
174. Miller, W. R. and G. S. Rose. *Toward a theory of motivational interviewing.* Am Psychol, 2009. **64**(6):527–37.
175. Miller, W. R. and S. Rollnick. *Motivational interviewing: Preparing people for change.* 2002, New York: Guilford Press.
176. Rollnick, S., W. R. Miller, and C. Butler. *Motivational interviewing in health care: Helping patients change behavior.* 2007, New York: Guilford Press.
177. Miller, W. R. *Rediscovering fire: Small interventions, large effects.* Psychology of Addictive Behaviors, 2000. **14**(1):6.
178. Kemp, B. *Quality of Life: What it really requires; How to get it and keep it.* 2012, Tustin, CA: Kemp.
179. Schultz, J. M., B. A. Tallman, and E. M. Altmaier. *Pathways to posttraumatic growth: The contributions of forgiveness and importance of religion and spirituality.* Psychology of Religion and Spirituality, 2010. **2**(2):104–14.
180. Gerber, M. M., A. Boals, and D. Schuettler. *The unique contributions of positive and negative religious coping to*

posttraumatic growth and PTSD. Psychology of Religion and Spirituality, 2011. **3**(4):298-307.

181. Currier, J. M. et al. *Bereavement, religion, and posttraumatic growth: A matched control group investigation.* Psychology of Religion and Spirituality, 2013. **5**(2):69-77.

182. Danhauer, S. C. et al. *A longitudinal investigation of posttraumatic growth in adult patients undergoing treatment for acute leukemia.* Journal of clinical psychology in medical settings, 2013. **20**(1):13-24.

183. Crick, F. *The Astonishing Hypothesis: The Scientific Search for the Soul.* 1994, New York: Charles Scribner's Sons. 317.

184. Willard, D. *A Place for Truth: Leading Thinkers Explore Life's Hardest Questions.* 2010, Downer's Grove, IL: InterVarsity Press.

185. Damasio, H. et al. *The return of Phineas Gage: Clues about the brain from the skull of a famous patient.* Science, 1994. **264**(5162):1102-05.

186. Brodmann, K. *Comparative Localization Studies in the Brain Cortex, its Fundamentals Represented on the Basis of its Cellular Architecture.* 1909, Leipzig, Germany: Johann Ambrosius Barth.

187. Ramon y Cajal, S. *Estudios sobre la degeneración y regeneración del sistema nervioso.* 1913, Madrid, Spain: Imprenta de hijos de Nicolás Moyá.

188. James, W. *The Laws of Habit.* The Popular Science Monthly, 1887:434.

189. Bracy, O. L. *Computer based cognitive rehabilitation.* Cognitive Rehabilitation, 1983. **Vol 1**(1):7-8, 18.

190. Bracy, O. L. *Cognitive rehabilitation: A process approach.* Cognitive Rehabilitation, 1986. **Vol 4**(2):10-17.

191. Hagen, C., D. Malkmus, and P. Durham. *Rancho Los Amigos Scale.* Communication Disorders Service, Rancho Los Amigos Hospital, 1972.
192. Bond, M. R. *The stages of recovery from severe head injury with special reference to late outcome.* Int Rehabil Med, 1979. **1**(4):155–59.
193. Taub, E., G. Uswatte, and T. Elbert. *New treatments in neurorehabilitation founded on basic research.* Nat Rev Neurosci, 2002. **3**(3):228–36.
194. Merzenich, M. M. et al. *Topographic reorganization of somatosensory cortical areas 3b and 1 in adult monkeys following restricted deafferentation.* Neuroscience, 1983. **8**(1):33–55.
195. Merzenich, M. et al. *Neural mechanisms underlying temporal integration, segmentation, and input sequence representation: Some implications for the origin of learning disabilities.* Annals New York Academy of Sciences, 1993:1–22.
196. Merzenich, M. et al. *Cortical plasticity underlying perceptual, motor, and cognitive skill development: Implications for neurorehabilitation.* Cold Spring Harb Symp Quant Biol, 1996. **61**:1–8.
197. Buonomano, D. and M. Merzenich. *Cortical plasticity: From synapses to maps.* Annual Review of Neuroscience, 1998. **21**:149–86.
198. Mahncke, H. W., A. Bronstone, and M. M. Merzenich. *Brain plasticity and functional losses in the aged: scientific bases for a novel intervention.* Prog Brain Res, 2006. **157**:81–109.
199. Mahncke, H. et al. *Memory enhancement in healthy older adults using a brain plasticity-based training program: A randomized, controlled study.* Proc Natl Acad Sci USA, 2006. **103**(33):12523–528.

200. Zhou, X. et al. *Natural restoration of critical period plasticity in the juvenile and adult primary auditory cortex.* J Neurosci, 2011. **31**(15):5625–634.
201. Maguire, E. et al. *Navigation-related structural change in the hippocampi of taxi drivers.* Proc Natl Acad Sci USA, 2000. **97**(8):4398–403.
202. Maguire, E., K. Woollett, and H. Spiers. *London taxi drivers and bus drivers: A structural MRI and neuropsychological analysis.* Hippocampus, 2006. **16**(12):1091–101.
203. Bach-y-Rita, P. *Sensory plasticity. Applications to a vision substitution system.* Acta Neurol Scand, 1967. **43**(4):417–26.
204. Bach-y-Rita, P. *Rehabilitation versus passive recovery of motor control following central nervous system lesions.* Adv Neurol, 1983. **39**:1085–92.
205. Bach-y-Rita, P. *Brain plasticity as a basis for recovery of function in humans.* Neuropsychologia, 1990. **28**(6):547–54.
206. Bach-y-Rita, P. *Theoretical and practical considerations in the restoration of function after stroke.* Top Stroke Rehabil, 2001. **8**(3): p. 1–15.
207. Bach-y-Rita, P. and E. W. Bach-y-Rita. *Biological and psychosocial factors in recovery from brain damage in humans.* Can J Psychol, 1990. **44**(2):148–65.
208. Taub, E. and G. Uswatte. *Use of CI therapy for improving motor ability after chronic CNS damage: A development prefigured by paul Bach-y-Rita.* Journal of Integrated Neuroscience, 2005. **4**(4):465–77.
209. Wolf, S. L. et al. *Effect of constraint-induced movement therapy on upper extremity function 3 to 9 months after stroke: the EXCITE randomized clinical trial.* JAMA, 2006. **296**(17):2095–104.

210. Taub, E. et al. *Method for enhancing real-world use of a more affected arm in chronic stroke: transfer package of constraint-induced movement therapy.* Stroke, 2013. **44**(5):1383–88.
211. Hoare, B. J. et al. *Constraint-induced movement therapy in the treatment of the upper limb in children with hemiplegic cerebral palsy.* Cochrane Database Syst Rev, 2007(2):CD004149.
212. Abd El-Kafy, E. M., S. A. Elshemy, and M. S. Alghamdi. *Effect of constraint-induced therapy on upper limb functions: A randomized control trial.* Scand J Occup Ther, 2014. **21**(1):11–23.
213. Wu, W. C. et al. *Group constraint-induced movement therapy for children with hemiplegic cerebral palsy: A pilot study.* American Journal of Occupational Therapy, 2013. **67**(2):201–08.
214. Pargament, K. I., J. J. Exline, and J. W. Jones, eds. *APA Handbook of Psychology, Religion, and Spirituality.* Vol. 1. 2013, Washington, DC: American Psychological Association.
215. Pargament, K. I., A. Mahoney, and E. P. Shafranske, eds. *APA Handbook of Psychology, Religion, and Spirituality.* Vol. 2. 2013, Washington, DC: American Psychological Association.
216. Hitchens, C. *God is not great: How religion poisons everything.* 2007, New York, NY: Hatchette Group.
217. Dawkins, R. *The god delusion.* 2006, Boston: Houghton Mifflin.
218. National Commission for the Protection of Human Subjects of Biomedical Behavioral Research. *The Belmont Report: Ethical principles and guidelines for the protection of human subjects of research.* 1978, Bethesda, MD: ERIC Clearinghouse.

219. Hubsch, C. et al. *Clinical classification of psychogenic non-epileptic seizures based on video-EEG analysis and automatic clustering.* Journal of Neurology, Neurosurgery & Psychiatry, 2011. **82**(9):955–60.
220. James, W. *What is an emotion?* Mind, 1884(34):188–205.
221. Cannon, W. B. *The interrelations of emotions as suggested by recent physiological researches.* The American Journal of Psychology, 1914:256–82.
222. Powley, T. L. *Central Control of Autonomic Funtion: Organization of the autonomic nervous system,* in *Fundamental Neuroscience,* L. R. Squire et al., eds. 2013, New York: Academic Press. 1127.
223. Cannon, W. B. *The Wisdom of the Body,* 1932, New York: W. W. Norton.
224. Cannon, W. B. *The James-Lange theory of emotions: A critical examination and an alternative theory.* The American Journal of Psychology, 1927. **39**(1/4):106–24.
225. Beck, A. *Depression: Causes and treatment.* 1967, Philadelphia: University of Pennsylvania.
226. Vögele, C. et al. *Cardiac autonomic regulation and anger coping in adolescents.* Biological psychology, 2010. **85**(3):465–71.
227. Vollmer-Conna, U. et al. *39. Vagus nerve activity, a good night's sleep, and recovery from acute infection.* Brain, Behavior, and Immunity, 2013. **32**:e11–e12.
228. Porges, S. W. *The polyvagal theory: Phylogenetic contributions to social behavior.* Physiology & Behavior, 2003. **79**(3):503–13.
229. Kemp, A. H. et al. *Impact of depression and antidepressant treatment on heart rate variability: A review and meta-analysis.* Biological Psychiatry, 2010. **67**(11):1067–74.
230. Billman, G. E. *Cardiac autonomic neural remodeling and susceptibility to sudden cardiac death: Effect of*

endurance exercise training. American Journal of Physiology-Heart and Circulatory Physiology, 2009. **297**(4):1171-93.
231. Pavlov, V. A. and K. J. Tracey. *The vagus nerve and the inflammatory reflex—linking immunity and metabolism.* Nature Reviews Endocrinology, 2012. **8**(12):743-54.
232. Elliott, R. E. et al. *Vagus nerve stimulation for children with treatment-resistant epilepsy: A consecutive series of 141 cases.* Journal of Neurosurgery: Pediatrics, 2011. **7**(5):491-500.
233. Borg, G. *Psychophysical bases of perceived exertion.* Med and Sci in Sports and Exercise, 1982. **14**(5):377-81.
234. Damasio, A. R. *The feeling of what happens: Body and emotion in the making of consciousness.* 2000, New York: Houghton Mifflin Harcourt.
235. Craig, A. *Interoception: The sense of the physiological condition of the body.* Current Opinion in Neurobiology, 2003. **13**(4):500-505.
236. Paul, M. and K. Garg. *The effect of heart rate variability biofeedback on performance psychology of basketball players.* Appl Psychophysiol Biofeedback, 2012. **37**(2):131-44.
237. Nolan, R. P. et al. *Heart rate variability biofeedback as a behavioral neurocardiac intervention to enhance vagal heart rate control.* American heart journal, 2005. **149**(6):1137.
238. Tan, G. et al. *Heart rate variability (HRV) and posttraumatic stress disorder (PTSD): A pilot study.* Applied Psychophysiology and Biofeedback, 2011. **36**(1):27-35.
239. Berry, M. E. et al. *Non-pharmacological Intervention for Chronic Pain in Veterans: A Pilot Study of Heart Rate*

Variability Biofeedback. Global Advances in Health and Medicine, 2014. **3**(2):28–33.
240. Kok, B. E. et al. *How Positive Emotions Build Physical Health Perceived Positive Social Connections Account for the Upward Spiral Between Positive Emotions and Vagal Tone.* Psychological science, 2013. **24**(7):1123–32.
241. Field, T. and M. Diego. *Vagal activity, early growth and emotional development.* Infant Behavior and Development, 2008. **31**(3):361–73.
242. Anderson, G. *Current knowledge about skin-to-skin (kangaroo) care for preterm infants.* Journal of perinatology: official journal of the California Perinatal Association, 1991. **11**(3):216–26.
243. Conde-Agudelo, A., J. Diaz-Rossello, and J. Belizan. *Kangaroo mother care to reduce morbidity and mortality in low birthweight infants.* Cochrane Database of Systematic Reviews, 2013(2):1–41.
244. Mitchell, A. et al. *Effects of daily kangaroo care on cardiorespiratory parameters in preterm infants.* Journal of neonatal-perinatal medicine, 2013. **6**(3):243-49.
245. Clark, W. M. *A legal background to the Yahwist's use of "Good and Evil" in Genesis 2–3.* Journal of Biblical Literature, 1969. 266–278.
246. Ito, T. A. et al. *Negative information weighs more heavily on the brain: The negativity bias in evaluative categorizations.* Journal of Personality and Social Psychology, 1998. **75**(4):887.
247. Holder, G. *Rooted: A journey through the book of James.* 2014, Chesterfield, MO: The Crossing.
248. Baslet, G. *Psychogenic non-epileptic seizures: A model of their pathogenic mechanism.* Seizure, 2011. **20**(1):1–13.

249. Poulose, S. M., M. G. Miller, and B. Shukitt-Hale. *Role of walnuts in maintaining brain health with age.* The Journal of Nutrition, 2014. **144**(4):561S-566S.
250. Choi, I.-Y. et al. *Association between dairy intake and brain glutathione levels in older adults.* The FASEB Journal, 2014. **28**(1 Supplement):1018.
251. Groves, N. J., J. J. McGrath, and T. H. Burne. *Vitamin D as a neurosteroid affecting the developing and adult brain.* Annual Review of Nutrition, 2014. **34**(August).
252. McAuley, E. et al. *Non-exercise estimated cardiorespiratory fitness: Associations with brain structure, cognition, and memory complaints in older adults.* Mental Health and Physical Activity, 2011. **4**(1):5-11.
253. Thurber, M. R. et al. *Effects of heart rate variability coherence biofeedback training and emotional management techniques to decrease music performance anxiety.* Biofeedback, 2010. **38**(1):28-40.
254. Sakakibara, M. et al. *Heart rate variability biofeedback improves cardiorespiratory resting function during sleep.* Psychophysiology and Biofeedback, 2013. **38**(4):265-71.
255. Lehrer, P. *History of heart rate variability biofeedback research: A personal and scientific voyage.* Biofeedback, 2013. **41**(3):88-97.
256. Cram, J. and T. Budzynski, *Biofeedback and relaxation therapies*, in *Interdisciplinary rehabilitation of low back pain*, C. Tollison and M. Kriegel, eds. 1989, Baltimore: Williams & Wilkins. 121-33.
257. von Dawans, B. et al. *The social dimension of stress reactivity acute stress increases prosocial behavior in humans.* Psychological Science, 2012. **23**(6):651-60.
258. Knafo, A. and R. Plomin. *Prosocial behavior from early to middle childhood: Genetic and environmental influences*

on stability and change. Developmental Psychology, 2006. **42**(5):771.
259. Kuiper, N. A. and R. A. Martin. *Laughter and stress in daily life: Relation to positive and negative affect.* Motivation and Emotion, 1998. **22**(2):133–53.
260. Riem, M. M. et al. *No laughing matter: Intranasal oxytocin administration changes functional brain connectivity during exposure to infant laughter.* Neuropsychopharmacology, 2012. **37**(5):1257–66.
261. Warren, R. *The purpose driven life: What on earth am I here for?* Expanded Edition ed. 2012, Grand Rapids, MI: Zondervan.
262. Bowlby, J. *The making and breaking of affectional bonds. I. Aetiology and psychopathology in the light of attachment theory.* The British Journal of Psychiatry, 1977. **130**(3):201–10.
263. Bowlby, J. *A secure base: Parent-child attachment and healthy human development.* 1988, London: Routledge.
264. Bretherton, I. *The origins of attachment theory: John Bowlby and Mary Ainsworth.* Developmental Psychology, 1992. **28**(5):759.
265. Johnson, S. M. and L. S. Greenberg. *Emotionally Focussed Couples Therapy: An outcome study.* Journal of Marital and Family Therapy, 1985. **11**(3):313–17.
266. Quirin, M. et al. *Adult attachment insecurity and hippocampal cell density.* Soc Cogn Affect Neurosci, 2010. **5**(1):39–47.
267. Atzil, S., T. Hendler, and R. Feldman. *Specifying the neurobiological basis of human attachment: Brain, hormones, and behavior in synchronous and intrusive mothers.* Neuropsychopharmacology, 2011. **36**(13):2603-15.

268. Donges, U. S. et al. *Adult attachment anxiety is associated with enhanced automatic neural response to positive facial expression.* Neuroscience, 2012. **220**:149–57.
269. Zhang, X. et al. *Can depression be diagnosed by response to mother's face? A personalized attachment-based paradigm for diagnostic fMRI.* PLoS One, 2011. **6**(12):e27253.
270. Ainsworth, M. D. *Infant-mother attachment.* American Psycholologist, 1979. **34**(10):932–37.
271. Fraley, R. C. et al. *Interpersonal and genetic origins of adult attachment styles: A longitudinal study from infancy to early adulthood.* J Pers Soc Psychol, 2013. **104**(5):817–38.
272. Fraley, R. C., G. I. Roisman, and J. D. Haltigan. *The legacy of early experiences in development: Formalizing alternative models of how early experiences are carried forward over time.* Dev Psychol, 2013. **49**(1):109–26.
273. Davidson, R. J. and B. S. McEwen. *Social influences on neuroplasticity: Stress and interventions to promote well-being.* Nature Neuroscience, 2012. **15**(5):689–95.
274. Fumagalli, F. et al. *Stress during development: Impact on neuroplasticity and relevance to psychopathology.* Progress in Neurobiology, 2007. **81**(4):197–217.
275. Baram, T. Z. et al. *Fragmentation and unpredictability of early life experience in mental disorders.* American Journal of Psychiatry, 2012. **169**(9):907–15.
276. Korosi, A. and T. Z. Baram. *The pathways from mother's love to baby's future.* Frontiers in Behavioral Neuroscience, 2009. **3**(27).
277. Cohen, D. *Probabilistic epigenesis: An alternative causal model for conduct disorders in children and adolescents.* Neuroscience & Biobehavioral Reviews, 2010. **34**(1):119–129.

278. Chung, W. C. and A. P. Auger. *Gender differences in neurodevelopment and epigenetics.* Pflügers Archiv-European Journal of Physiology, 2013. **465**(5):573-84.
279. Vastag, B. *Scientists find connections in the brain between physical and emotional pain.* JAMA, 2003. **290**(18):2389-90.
280. Kross, E. et al. *Social rejection shares somatosensory representations with physical pain.* Proceedings of the National Academy of Sciences, 2011. **108**(15):6270-75.
281. Meerwijk, E. L., J. M. Ford, and S. J. Weiss. *Brain regions associated with psychological pain: Implications for a neural network and its relationship to physical pain.* Brain Imaging and Behavior, 2012. **7**(1):1-14.
282. Waters, E. et al. *Attachment security in infancy and early adulthood: A twenty-year longitudinal study.* Child development, 2000. **71**(3):684-89.
283. Bouvette-Turcot, A.A. et al. *Intergenerational transmission of psychosocial risk: Maternal childhood adversity, mother-child attachment, and child temperament.* Psychologica Belgica, 2013. **53**(3): p. 65-83.
284. Galynker, I. I. et al. *Distinct but overlapping neural networks subserve depression and insecure attachment.* Social Cognitive and Affective Neuroscience, 2012. **7**(8):896-908.
285. Zhang, X. et al. *Can depression be diagnosed by response to mother's face? A personalized attachment-based paradigm for diagnostic fMRI.* PloS one, 2011. **6**(12):e27253.
286. Lenzi, D. et al. *Attachment models affect brain responses in areas related to emotions and empathy in nulliparous women.* Human Brain Mapping, 2013. **34**(6):1399-1414.
287. Schneider, S. et al. *Maternal interpersonal affiliation is associated with adolescents' brain structure and*

reward processing. Translational psychiatry, 2012. **2**(11):e182.
288. Willard, D. *The Divine Conspiracy, Rediscovering Our Hidden Life in God*, 1998, San Francisco: HarperCollins.
289. Willard, D. *The Genius of Jesus*, in *Veritas Forum* 2013: Ohio State University.
290. Strathearn, L. et al. *Adult attachment predicts maternal brain and oxytocin response to infant cues.* Neuropsychopharmacology, 2009. **34**(13):2655–66.
291. Karremans, J. C. et al. *Secure attachment partners attenuate neural responses to social exclusion: An fMRI investigation.* International Journal of Psychophysiology, 2011. **81**(1):44–50.
292. Schore, A. N. *Effects of a secure attachment relationship on right brain development, affect regulation, and infant mental health.* Infant Mental Health Journal, 2001. **22**(1):7–66.
293. Willard, D. and J. Ortberg. *Living in Christ's Presence: Final Words on Heaven and the Kingdom of God.* 2013, Downser's Grove, IL: InterVarsity Press.
294. Seltzer, L. J., T. E. Ziegler, and S. D. Pollak. *Social vocalizations can release oxytocin in humans.* Proc Biol Sci, 2010. **277**(1694):2661–66.
295. Schneiderman, I. et al. *Oxytocin during the initial stages of romantic attachment: Relations to couples' interactive reciprocity.* Psychoneuroendocrinology, 2012. **37**(8):1277–85.
296. Lee, H. J. et al. *Oxytocin: the great facilitator of life.* Prog Neurobiol, 2009. **88**(2):127–51.
297. Strathearn, L. *Maternal neglect: Oxytocin, dopamine and the neurobiology of attachment.* Journal of Neuroendocrinology, 2011. **23**(11):1054–65.

298. Uvnas-Moberg, K. *Short-term and long-term effects of oxytocin released by suckling and of skin-to-skin contact in mothers and infants.* Evolution, Early Experience and Human Development: From Research to Practice and Policy. 2013, New York: Oxford University Press.
299. Cardoso, C. et al. *Intranasal oxytocin attenuates the cortisol response to physical stress: a dose-response study.* Psychoneuroendocrinology, 2013. **38**(3):399–407.
300. Linnen, A. M. et al. *Intranasal oxytocin and salivary cortisol concentrations during social rejection in university students.* Stress, 2012. **15**(4):393–402.
301. Leuner, B., J. M. Caponiti, and E. Gould. *Oxytocin stimulates adult neurogenesis even under conditions of stress and elevated glucocorticoids.* Hippocampus, 2012. **22**(4):861–68.
302. Labuschagne, I. et al. *Oxytocin attenuates amygdala reactivity to fear in generalized social anxiety disorder.* Neuropsychopharmacology, 2010. **35**(12):2403–13.
303. Clow, A. et al. *The cortisol awakening response: More than a measure of HPA axis function.* Neuroscience & Biobehavioral Reviews, 2010. **35**(1):97–103.
304. Zeitzer, J. M. *Control of sleep and wakefulness in health and disease.* Prog Mol Biol Transl Sci, 2013. **119**:137–54.
305. Sapolsky, R. M. et al. *Why zebras don't get ulcers.* 2004: Times Books New York.
306. Miller, G. E., E. Chen, and E. S. Zhou. *If it goes up, must it come down? Chronic stress and the hypothalamic-pituitary-adrenocortical axis in humans.* Psychological Bulletin, 2007. **133**(1):25–45.
307. Pagliaccio, D. et al. *Stress-system genes and life stress predict cortisol levels and amygdala and hippocampal volumes in children.* Neuropsychopharmacology, 2014. **39**:1245–53.

308. Karelina, K. and A. C. DeVries. *Modeling social influences on human health.* Psychosomatic Medicine, 2011. **73**(1):67–74.
309. Broadbent, E. and H. E. Koschwanez. *The psychology of wound healing.* Curr Opin Psychiatry, 2012. **25**(2):135–40.
310. Rash, J. A., A. Aguirre-Camacho, and T. S. Campbell. *Oxytocin and Pain: A systematic review and synthesis of findings.* Clinical Journal of Pain, 2014. **30**(5):453–62.
311. De Dreu, C. K. et al. *Oxytonergic circuitry sustains and enables creative cognition in humans.* Social cognitive and affective neuroscience, 2013.
312. Evans, S., S. S. Shergill, and B. B. Averbeck. *Oxytocin decreases aversion to angry faces in an associative learning task.* Neuropsychopharmacology, 2010. **35**(13):2502–09.
313. Petrovic, P. et al. *Oxytocin attenuates affective evaluations of conditioned faces and amygdala activity.* J Neurosci, 2008. **28**(26):6607–15.
314. Kemp, A. H. et al. *Oxytocin increases heart rate variability in humans at rest: Implications for social approach-related motivation and capacity for social engagement.* PLoS One, 2012. **7**(8).
315. Nation, D. A. et al. *Oxytocin Attenuates Atherosclerosis and Adipose Tissue Inflammation in Socially Isolated ApoE-/- Mice.* Psychosomatic Medicine, 2010. **72**(4):376–82.
316. Buchheim, A. et al. *Oxytocin enhances the experience of attachment security.* Psychoneuroendocrinology, 2009. **34**(9):1417–22.
317. Galbally, M. et al. *The role of oxytocin in mother-infant relations: A systematic review of human studies.* Harvard Review of Psychiatry, 2011. **19**(1):1–14.

318. Riem, M. M. et al. *Oxytocin effects on complex brain networks are moderated by experiences of maternal love withdrawal.* European Neuropsychopharmacology, 2013. **23**(10):1288–95.
319. Yamasue, H. et al. *Integrative approaches utilizing oxytocin to enhance prosocial behavior: From animal and human social behavior to autistic social dysfunction.* Journal of Neuroscience, 2012. **32**(41):14109–17.
320. Zink, C. F. and A. Meyer-Lindenberg. *Human neuroimaging of oxytocin and vasopressin in social cognition.* Horm Behav, 2012. **61**(3):400–09.
321. Rault, J. L. et al. *Repeated intranasal oxytocin administration in early life dysregulates the HPA axis and alters social behavior.* Physiol Behav, 2013. **112-113C**:40–48.
322. Sripada, C. S. et al. *Oxytocin enhances resting-state connectivity between amygdala and medial frontal cortex.* The International Journal of Neuropsychopharmacology, 2013. **16**(02):255–60.
323. Beetz, A. et al. *Psychosocial and psychophysical effects of human-animal interactions: The possible role of oxytocin.* Frontiers in Psychology, 2012. **3**(234).
324. Schore, A. N. *The effects of early relational trauma on right brain development, affect regulation, and infant mental health.* Infant Mental Health Journal, 2001. **22**(1):201–69.
325. Hanson, J. L. et al. *Early neglect is associated with alterations in white matter integrity and cognitive functioning.* Child Development, 2013. **84**(5):1566–78.
326. Teicher, M. H. et al. *Childhood neglect is associated with reduced corpus callosum area.* Biological Psychiatry, 2004. **56**(2):80–85.

327. Dannlowski, U. et al. *Limbic scars: Long-term consequences of childhood maltreatment revealed by functional and structural magnetic resonance imaging.* Biological Psychiatry, 2012. **71**(4):286–93.
328. Sheridan, M. A. et al. *Variation in neural development as a result of exposure to institutionalization early in childhood.* Proceedings of the National Academy of Sciences, 2012. **109**(32):12927–932.
329. Cohn, A. *Child of Rage: A Story of Abuse*, in HBO America Undercover 1990.
330. Robles, T. F. et al. *Marital quality and health: A meta-analytic review.* Psychological Bulletin, 2014. **140**(1):140–87.
331. Johnson, N. J. et al. *Marital status and mortality: the national longitudinal mortality study.* Annals of epidemiology, 2000. **10**(4):224–38.
332. Orth-Gomer, K. et al. *Marital stress worsens prognosis in women with coronary heart disease: The Stockholm Female Coronary Risk Study.* JAMA, 2000. **284**(23):3008–14.
333. Robles, T. F. and J. K. Kiecolt-Glaser. *The physiology of marriage: Pathways to health.* Physiology & Behavior, 2003. **79**(3):409–16.
334. Ditzen, B., C. Hoppmann, and P. Klumb. *Positive couple interactions and daily cortisol: On the stress-protecting role of intimacy.* Psychosomatic Medicine, 2008. **70**(8): 883–89.
335. Heffner, K. L. et al. *Spousal support satisfaction as a modifier of physiological responses to marital conflict in younger and older couples.* Journal of Behavioral Medicine, 2004. **27**(3):233–54.

336. Saxbe, D. E., R. L. Repetti, and A. Nishina. *Marital satisfaction, recovery from work, and diurnal cortisol among men and women.* Health Psychology, 2008. **27**(1):15.
337. Slatcher, R. B. et al. *Momentary work worries, marital disclosure, and salivary cortisol among parents of young children.* Psychosomatic Medicine, 2010. **72**(9):887–96.
338. Liu, S. et al. *Synchrony of diurnal cortisol pattern in couples.* Journal of Family Psychology, 2013. **27**(4):579.
339. Papp, L. M. et al. *Spouses' cortisol associations and moderators: Testing physiological synchrony and connectedness in everyday life.* Family Process, 2013. **52**(2):284–98.
340. Saxbe, D. and R. L. Repetti. *For better or worse? Coregulation of couples' cortisol levels and mood states.* Journal of personality and social psychology, 2010. **98**(1):92.
341. Delaney, H. D., W. R. Miller, and A. M. Bisonó. *Religiosity and spirituality among psychologists: A survey of clinician members of the American Psychological Association.* Spirituality in Clinical Practice, 2013. **1**(S):95–106.
342. Gregory, D. *Dinner with a Perfect Stranger: An Invitation Worth Considering.* 2011, Colorado Springs, CO: WaterBrook Press.
343. Manning, B. *Abba's Child: The cry of the heart for intimate belonging.* 2002, Colorado Springs: Navpress. 192.
344. Mandino, O. *The Greatest Miracle in the World.* 1975, Hollywood, FL: Fredrick Fell.
345. Lewis, C. S. *Mere Christianity.* 1952, London: C. S. Lewis.
346. Young, W. *The Shack.* 2007, Los Angeles: Windblown Media. 254.
347. Galton, F. *Statistical inquiries into the efficacy of prayer.* Fortnightly Review, 1872. **12**:125–35.

348. Freud, S. and W.D.R. Scott. *The Future of an Illusion: Translated by WD Robson-Scott*. 1928: Institute of Psycho-Analysis: London.
349. Myers, D. G. *The funds, friends, and faith of happy people*. American Psychologist, 2000. **55**(1): p. 56.
350. Diener, E., L. Tay, and D. G. Myers. *The religion paradox: If religion makes people happy, why are so many dropping out?* Journal of Personality and Social Psychology, 2011. **101**(6).
351. Miller, W. R. and C. E. Thoresen. *Spirituality, religion, and health: An emerging research field*. American Psychologist, 2003. **58**(1):24.
352. Powell, L. H., L. Shahabi, and C. E. Thoresen. *Religion and spirituality: Linkages to physical health*. American Psychologist, 2003. **58**(1):36.
353. Koenig, H. *Religion, spirituality, and health: The research and clinical implications*. ISRN Psychiatry, 2012. **2012**.
354. McCullough, M. E. et al. *Religious involvement and mortality: A meta-analytic review*. Health Psychology, 2000. **19**(3):211–22.
355. Hummer, R. A. et al. *Religious involvement and US adult mortality*. Demography, 1999. **36**(2):273–85.
356. Koenig, H., D. E. King, and V. B. Carson, eds. *Handbook of Religion and Health*. 2nd ed. 2012, New York: Oxford University Press.
357. Bonelli, R. M. and H. G. Koenig. *Mental disorders, religion and spirituality 1990 to 2010: A systematic evidence-based review*. Journal of Religion and Health, 2013. **52**(2):657–73.
358. Tedeschi, R. G. and R. J. McNally. *Can we facilitate posttraumatic growth in combat veterans?* American Psychologist, 2011. **66**(1):19.

359. Calhoun, L. G., A. Cann, and R. G. Tedeschi. *The posttraumatic growth model: Sociocultural considerations*. Posttraumatic growth and culturally competent practice: Lessons learned from around the globe, 2010. 1–14.
360. Koenig, H. *Religious versus conventional psychotherapy for major depression in patients with chronic medical illness: Rationale, methods, and preliminary results*. Depression Research and Treatment, 2012. **2012**:460419.
361. Boyle, G., *Tattoos on the Heart*. 2010, New York: Free Press.
362. Buckner, R. L., J. R. Andrews-Hanna, and D. L. Schacter. *The brain's default network*. Annals of the New York Academy of Sciences, 2008. **1124**(1):1–38.
363. Spreng, R. N. and C. L. Grady. *Patterns of brain activity supporting autobiographical memory, prospection, and theory of mind, and their relationship to the default mode network*. Journal of Cognitive Neuroscience, 2010. **22**(6):1112–23.
364. Greicius, M. D. et al. *Resting-state functional connectivity reflects structural connectivity in the default mode network*. Cerebral Cortex, 2009. **19**(1):72–78.
365. Raichle, M. E. and A. Z. Snyder. *A default mode of brain function: A brief history of an evolving idea*. NeuroImage, 2007. **37**(4):1083–90.
366. Fair, D. A. et al. *The maturing architecture of the brain's default network*. Proceedings of the National Academy of Sciences, 2008. **105**(10):4028–32.
367. Avram, M. et al. *Neurofunctional correlates of esthetic and moral judgments*. Neuroscience Letters, 2013. **534**(0):128–32.
368. Feldman Hall, O. et al. *Differential neural circuitry and self-interest in real vs hypothetical moral decisions*. Social Cognitive and Affective Neuroscience, 2012. **7**(7):743–51.

369. Menon, V. *Large-scale brain networks and psychopathology: A unifying triple network model.* Trends in Cognitive Sciences, 2011. **15**(10):483–506.
370. Seeley, W. W., J. Zhou, and E.-J. Kim. *Frontotemporal dementia: What can the behavioral variant teach us about human brain organization?* The Neuroscientist, 2012. **18**(4):373–85.
371. Sheline, Y. I. et al. *The default mode network and self-referential processes in depression.* Proceedings of the National Academy of Sciences, 2009. **106**(6):1942–47.
372. Broyd, S. J. et al. *Default-mode brain dysfunction in mental disorders: A systematic review.* Neuroscience & Biobehavioral Reviews, 2009. **33**(3):279–96.
373. Harrison, B. J. et al. *Neural correlates of moral sensitivity in obsessive-compulsive disorder: Moral sensitivity in obsessive-compulsive disorder.* Archives of General Psychiatry, 2012. **69**(7):741–49.
374. Inzlicht, M., A. M. Tullett, and M. Good. *The need to believe: A neuroscience account of religion as a motivated process.* Religion, Brain & Behavior, 2011. **1**(3):192–212.
375. Brown, B. *The gifts of imperfection: Let go of who you think you're supposed to be and embrace who you are.* 2010, Center City, MN: Hazelden Publishing.
376. Holder, G. *On the Edge*, 2012, Chesterfield, MO: The Crossing Church.
377. Newton, J. and W. Cowper. *Amazing Grace*, in *Olney Hymns* 1779: Olney, Buckinghamshire ,England.
378. Perls, F. S. *Gestalt Therapy Verbatim.* 1969, Lafayette, CA: Real People Press. 279.
379. Popper, K. *The Logic of Scientific Discovery.* 2002, London: Routledge.

380. Hyde, J. S. *The gender similarities hypothesis.* American Psychologist, 2005. **60**(6).
381. Matheson, L. N. et al. *Age and gender normative data for lift capacity.* Work: A Journal of Prevention, Assessment and Rehabilitation, 2013.
382. Sarkar, S. et al. *Frontotemporal white-matter microstructural abnormalities in adolescents with conduct disorder: a diffusion tensor imaging study.* Psychol Med, 2013. **43**(2): 401–11.
383. Fairchild, G. et al. *Brain structure abnormalities in adolescent girls with conduct disorder.* J Child Psychol Psychiatry, 2013. **54**(1):86–95.
384. Diamond, L. M. and M. R. Cribbet. *Links between adolescent sympathetic and parasympathetic nervous system functioning and interpersonal behavior over time.* International Journal of Psychophysiology, 2013. **88**(3):339–348.
385. Owens, E. W. et al. *The impact of internet pornography on adolescents: A review of the research.* Sexual Addiction & Compulsivity, 2012. **19**(1–2):99–122.
386. Yaxley, R. H. et al. *Behavioral risk elicits selective activation of the executive system in adolescents: Clinical implications.* Frontiers in Psychiatry, 2011. **2**.
387. Matheson, L. *History, design characteristics, and uses of the pictorial activity and task sorts.* Journal of Occupational Rehabilitation, 2004. **14**(3):175–95.
388. Gillham, J. et al. *Character strengths predict subjective well-being during adolescence.* The Journal of Positive Psychology, 2011. **6**(1):31–44.
389. Peterson, C. et al. *Strengths of character and posttraumatic growth.* J Trauma Stress, 2008. **21**(2):214–17.

390. Jackson, J., D. A. Balota, and D. Head. *Exploring the relationship between personality and regional brain volume in healthy aging.* Neurobiology of Aging, 2011. **32**(12):2162-71.
391. Hannah, S. T. and B. J. Avolio. *Moral potency: Building the capacity for character-based leadership.* Consulting Psychology Journal: Practice and Research, 2010. **62**(4).
392. Hannah, S. T., B. J. Avolio, and D. R. May. *Moral maturation and moral conation: A capacity approach to explaining moral thought and action.* Academy of Management Review, 2011. **36**(4):663-85.
393. Sosik, J. J. and J. C. Cameron. *Character and authentic transformational leadership behavior: Expanding the ascetic self toward others.* Consulting Psychology Journal: Practice and Research, 2010. **62**(4):251.
394. Hannah, S. T., B. J. Avolio, and F. O. Walumbwa. *Relationships between authentic leadership, moral courage, and ethical and pro-social behaviors.* Business Ethics Quarterly, 2011. **21**(4):555-78.
395. Allman, I. and P. J. Magistretti. *Brain Energy Metabolism*, in *Fundamental Neuroscience*, L. R. Squire et al., eds. 2013, New York: Academic Press. 1127.
396. Fields, R. D. *The Other Brain.* 2009, New York: Simon & Schuster.
397. Greenemeier, L. *Computers have a lot to learn from the human brain.* Scientific American Blog 2009 November 4, 2013; available from www.scientificamerican.com/blog.
398. McCrory, P. et al. *Consensus statement on concussion in sport.* British Journal of Sports Medicine, 2013. **47**(5):250-58.
399. Silverberg, N. D. and G. L. Iverson. *Is rest after concussion "the best medicine?": Recommendations for*

activity resumption following concussion in athletes, civilians, and military service members. The Journal of Head Trauma Rehabilitation, 2013. **28**(4):250–59.

400. Peak, D. and M. Frame. *Chaos Under Control: The Art and Science of Complexity.* 1994, New York: W. H. Freeman.

401. Rohr, R. *Falling upward: A spirituality for the two halves of life.* 2011: Wiley. com.

402. Berkers, R. M. and M. T. van Kesteren. *Autobiographical memory transformation across consolidation.* The Journal of Neuroscience, 2013. **33**(13):5435–36.

403. Simpson, J. A. and E. S. Weiner. *The Oxford English Dictionary.* Vol. 2. 1989, Oxford: Clarendon Press.

404. Lewis, C. S. *Letters to Malcolm: Chiefly on prayer.* 2002, New York: Houghton Mifflin Harcourt.

405. Lewis, C. S. *Surprised by joy: The shape of my early life.* 1955, New York: Houghton Mifflin Harcourt.

406. Warren, K. *Choose Joy: Because Happiness Isn't Enough.* 2012: Baker Books.

407. Warren, R. and K. Warren. *How to Get Through What You're Going Through,* 2013, Saddleback Church: El Toro, CA.

408. Carver, C. S., M. F. Scheier, and S. C. Segerstrom. *Optimism.* Clinical Psychology Review, 2010. **30**(7):879–89.

409. Kim, E. S., N. Park, and C. Peterson. *Dispositional optimism protects older adults from stroke: The Health and Retirement Study.* Stroke, 2011. **42**(10):2855–59.

410. Sharot, T. *The optimism bias.* Current Biology, 2011. **21**(23):R941–R945.

411. Shizgal, P. and S. Hyman. *Homeostasis, Motivation, and Addictive States,* in *Principles of Neural Science,*

E. Kandel et al. Editors. 2013, New York: McGraw Hill Medical. 1095-15.
412. Lee, W. and J. Reeve. *Self-determined, but not non-self-determined, motivation predicts activations in the anterior insular cortex: An fMRI study of personal agency.* Social Cognitive and Affective Neuroscience, 2013. **8**(5):538-45.
413. Lee, W. et al. *Neural differences between intrinsic reasons for doing versus extrinsic reasons for doing: An fMRI study.* Neuroscience Research, 2012. **73**(1):68-72.
414. Peterson, C. *A Primer in Positive Psychology.* 2006, Oxford: Oxford University Press.
415. Matheson, L. *Goaling Process: Aging with a disability*, 1976: University of Southern California Ethel Percy Andrus Gerontology Center.
416. Wright, N. T. *After you believe: Why Christian character matters.* 2010: Grand Rapids, MI: Zondervan.
417. Author, *The Big Book.* 4th ed. 2001, New York: Alcoholics Anonymous World Services.

Index

A

acetylcholine 195
acupuncture 198
addiction 198, 201
adrenal glands, 199
adrenaline. *See* epinephrine
aggression 195
alcohol 206
Alcoholics Anonymous 65, 105, 193
alertness 199
Amazing Grace 148
American Psychological Association 87
amphetamine 206
amygdala 67, 96, 121, 195, 200, 201, 204
anger 195
anterior cingulate cortex 144, 195
anticipation 195, 203
antidepressant medication 127
anxiety 202, 203
anxiety disorder 23, 98
appetite 204
arousal 202
attachment 87, 104, 105, 122, 142, 201
attention 69, 201, 202
attentiveness 195, 198
attitudes 33, 155, 157, 158, 159, 161
autism 102, 122, 123, 202
autobiographical memory 200
autonomic balance 145
autonomic nervous system 32, 100, 106, 146, 195, 201
axon 196, 203, 205

B

Bach-y-Rita family 86
basal ganglia 197
Baumgartner, Thomas 33
BBCC. *See* Brain-Based Christian Counseling
Beck, Aaron 97, 101
behavioral flexibility 202
beliefs 33, 128, 157, 174
Beta-endorphin 198
Bible 8, 19, 24, 32, 42, 60, 61, 62, 63, 64, 65, 76, 86, 88, 103, 105, 140, 141, 158, 172, 173, 191
biofeedback 101, 108
blood pressure 199, 201
body temperature 204
borderline personality disorder 122
Boyle, Father Gregory 138
Brain-Based Christian Counseling 43, 67, 138, 140
brain energy 164
brain-restorative sleep 43, 69, 203
brainstem 195, 196
breast-feeding 198
breathing 196
Brocas area 78
Brodmann, Korbinian 79
Brown, Brené 145
Brown, Warren 174
Burdine, Richard 135

C

Cannon, Walter 96, 97
Carter, Sue 33
catecholamines 196

CBT. *See* cognitive behavior therapy
central nervous system 197
cerebellum 196
cerebral cortex 32, 67, 76, 78, 95, 96, 97, 99, 141, 142, 157, 159, 196, 197, 199, 200, 201, 203, 204, 205, 206
cerebrum 196, 197, 205
character 7, 12, 26, 45, 46, 146, 156, 158, 159, 160, 174, 183, 185, 192
childhood neglect 124
chili peppers 198
chocolate 198
choices 11, 12, 45, 74, 136, 137, 140, 142, 144, 153, 155, 157, 158, 192
Christianity 19, 129, 157, 179
cingulate cortex 197
circadian rhythm 201, 202, 205
cocaine 198, 206
cognitive behavior therapy 67, 98, 108, 138, 140
cognitive efficiency 164
Collins, Francis 87
Comprehensive Soldier Fitness 65
connectome 27
consilience xv, 11, 71
constraint-induced movement therapy 85
contract marriage 128
coping 87
corpus callosum 195, 196, 197
corrective emotions 42, 136, 137, 140, 142, 144, 146
cortisol 121, 122, 123, 125, 146, 204, 205
covenant 62
Cozolino, Louis 33

D

Damasio, Antonio and Hanna 33
decision-making 195, 204, 206
Default Mode Network 144
dementia 131
dendrite 197, 203, 205
dentate gyrus 197

depression 12, 23, 40, 97, 98, 101, 102, 122, 125, 127, 138, 144, 183, 186, 198, 202, 203, 204
desire 157, 178
digestion 196
discernment 204
disciples 25, 62, 64, 65
DMN 144
dopamine 196, 198, 206
Dr. Bob 105

E

Eberle, Elizabeth 3
embarrassment 10, 42, 136, 137, 140, 141, 145, 146, 148
emotion 201, 204, 205
emotional awareness 201
emotional inhibition 202
emotional salience 51, 58, 59, 60, 61, 62, 63, 71, 72, 141, 197, 201, 203
emotional tone 202
emotions 201
empathy 195, 202
endocrine system 201
endorphin 198
enteric nervous system 196
entorhinal cortex 198
epigenesis 23, 24, 74, 75, 177, 178, 186
epinephrine 196, 199
episodic-autobiographical memory 195
error-related negativity 144
evil 63, 87, 103, 146, 178
executive function 199
exercise 63, 69, 125, 198
experience-dependent plasticity 21
eye-pupil dilation 196

F

faith xi, 2, 6, 9, 11, 43, 62, 69, 71, 76, 86, 87, 88, 124, 131, 132, 138, 143, 147, 153, 159, 172, 178, 189
faithful brain 12, 13, 28, 41, 49, 63, 71, 106, 140, 146, 148, 174, 177, 180, 192, 193

faithful brain fitness xvi
Faithful Brain Fitness Assessment 13
family values 7
Father Bob 6, 9, 12
fatigue 201
fear 206
fight-flight-or-freeze 145, 195, 196
float tank relaxation 198
free will 12, 166
frontal lobe 199, 201, 204
fusiform face area 199
future consequences 206

G

GABA 199
Gage, Phineas 76
gamma-aminobutyric acid 199
gastrointestinal system 196, 199
Gazzaniga, Michael 33
gender-specific social cues 206
Gipson 6. See Father Bob
glial cells 199
glutamate 199
Goaling 44, 189
goals 7, 82, 157, 158, 180, 186, 187, 189, 190, 191
God-reflecting virtues 158
Gods created reality xv, 10, 13, 24, 34, 48, 63, 64, 74, 140, 151, 158, 159, 191
Godzillion 165
grace 42, 74, 105, 137, 138, 139, 140, 141, 142, 143, 145, 146, 147, 148, 152, 154, 158, 184
gratitude 43, 44, 108
gray matter 196
Gregory, David 128
guilt 10, 42, 136, 140, 146, 148

H

habits 24, 98, 178
Happy Hippocampus Exercise 45, 46, 200, 203
heart 7, 25, 32, 48, 64, 90, 97, 99, 100, 101, 102, 104, 105, 106, 122, 130, 141, 144, 147, 158, 179, 183, 185, 195, 203

heart rate 196
heart rate variability 99, 101, 102
Hebb, Donald O. 81
heroin 198, 206
hippocampal rehearsal 40, 42, 45, 200
hippocampus 46, 67, 95, 96, 97, 98, 122, 197, 198, 200, 201
Holder, Greg xi, 11
Holy Spirit 64, 106, 129, 172, 173, 174, 177
homeostasis 94, 98, 100, 199
homework 46, 47, 108
horizontal integration 33, 49, 61
hormone 125, 166, 196, 198, 199, 201, 205
hunger 201
hypothalamus 97, 120, 201, 204, 205

I

impulse control 195
instinctive behavior 201
institutional review board 88
insular cortex 201
integration, neuroscience and Scripture 10
intentionality 202
interpersonal neurobiology 33
Islam 19

J

James, William 80, 83, 93
Jeeves, Malcolm 174
Jesus xi, 2, 8, 11, 12, 24, 26, 32, 33, 45, 61, 62, 63, 64, 65, 74, 75, 104, 106, 109, 128, 129, 139, 140, 141, 143, 145, 146, 151, 152, 153, 154, 155, 156, 157, 158, 159, 161, 172, 174, 177, 178, 182, 183, 185, 191, 192
joy 180, 186
Judaism 19
judgment 204
just-right challenge 81, 151, 152

K

Kaas, Jon 82, 86
kangaroo care 103
Kemp, Bryan 181, 208
keystone habit 43
Kirkland, Russ 20, 132, 207

L

lactation 198
language 205
learning 197, 199, 201, 203
Lewis, C.S. 63, 128, 182
limbic system 32, 61, 95, 97, 98, 99, 141, 142, 156, 159, 195, 197, 201, 203
locus ceruleus 201, 203
logical speech. 201
long-term memory 200
Lybarger, Matt 208

M

Mandino, Og 128
Manning, Brennan 128
marijuana 206
marriage 124, 125, 152
meditation 87
medulla oblongata 195
melatonin 202, 205
memories 205
memory 195, 197, 199, 201, 202, 204
Merzenich, Michael 82, 86
methamphetamine 198
Miller, William 66
mind 11, 12, 25, 32, 48, 74, 75, 83, 130, 158, 176, 179, 202
mirror neuron 202
mood 204
moral decisions 205
moral inventory 117
morality 33
morphine 198
motivation 198, 201, 203
Munday, Danny 178
myelin 196

N

National Institutes of Health 87
nausea 198
navigation 204
neocortex 196, 198
neural networks 11, 12, 24, 46, 157, 202
neural patterns 24, 96, 142, 156, 166, 172, 174
neurochemicals 166
neuroconsolidation 43, 173, 200, 202
neurogenesis 24, 74, 75, 122, 177, 178, 186, 197, 199
neuron 122, 196, 197, 199, 202, 203
neuropeptide 120, 204
neuroplasticity 24, 46, 74, 75, 80, 81, 82, 83, 85, 86, 87, 88, 145, 156, 166, 174, 177, 178, 186, 192, 202, 203
neurorehabilitation 1, 2, 5, 6, 7, 8, 13, 24, 75, 81, 85, 86, 88, 106, 192
neuroscience xi, 2, 6, 10, 11, 24, 26, 64, 74, 75, 76, 82, 86, 103, 104, 106, 124, 130, 192
neurotransmitter 195, 198, 199, 204
neurovisceral integration 32
new covenant love 147
Newton, Captain John 148
nicotine 206
Nietzsche, Friedrich 151
noradrenaline. *See* norepinephrine
norepinephrine 196, 201, 203
nucleus accumbens 203, 206
nutrition 69

O

obedience 174
obsessive-compulsive disorder 122
occipital lobe 203, 204
olfactory bulb 197
opiates 206
optic chiasm 205
optic nerve 202
optimism 47, 186, 188

optogenetic 27
orbitofrontal cortex 204
oxytocin 120, 122, 123, 145, 204

P

panic 201
panic disorder 202, 203
parables 64
parasympathetic nervous system 100, 145, 196
parenting 201
parietal lobe 204
Parkinsons disease 20
Paul, the Apostle 12, 74, 75, 83, 87, 88, 177, 178, 182, 191, 193
peripheral nervous system 195
Perls, Fritz 150
Personal Prayer Relaxation 43, 67, 69, 108
perspiration 196
physiological arousal 69
pineal gland 202, 205
pituitary 97, 120, 201, 204
placenta 198
Plaza Towers Elementary School 56
polyvagal nervous system 32
Porges, Stephen 32, 99
pornography 24
positive affect 47
positive psychology 46, 200
post-traumatic growth 132
post-traumatic stress disorder 40, 53, 59, 98
prayer 10, 33, 41, 42, 43, 44, 67, 69, 101, 106, 108
prefrontal cortex 160, 206
Prodigal Son 8
psychogenic non-epileptic seizure 106
PTSD. See post-traumatic stress disorder

R

Ramón y Cajal, Santiago 80
Rancho Los Amigos 2, 6, 81, 178
Reboot Combat Recovery 56
redemption 3, 11, 13, 26, 104, 106, 136, 140, 142, 143, 191, 193
regret 136
rehabilitation 3, 11, 13, 26, 41, 76, 82, 85, 142, 143
religion 87
resilience 11, 47, 49, 66, 69, 70, 99
reward 203
reward network, 198
reward system 203
risks and rewards 206
Rogers, Carl 65
Rohr, Richard 172

S

Saddleback Church 10, 182
salivation 196
Saul of Tarsus 177
schizophrenia 23, 99, 122
Scripture 144
self-awareness 201
self-efficacy 46
self-narrative 46
self-other distinction 205
sense of smell 201
serotonin 145, 204
sexual gratification 198
sexuality 195
shame 10, 40, 42, 136, 137, 139, 140, 141, 145, 146, 148
short-term memory 200
Siegel, Daniel 33
sin 19, 23, 25, 42, 47, 48, 104, 139
Skinner, B.F. 81
sleep 201, 202, 204
sleep-wake cycle 202
social anxiety disorder 122
social engagement system 32
social integration 33, 49
soul 25, 48, 104, 137, 158, 166, 179
spatial navigation 200
spatial sense 204
Sperry, Roger 33
spiritual discipline 24
spirituality 87, 131, 132, 174

split-brain research 33
statistics 154
stem cells 197, 199
stress 87, 201, 202
subjective units of distress scale 68
substantia nigra 198
suprachiasmatic nucleus 202, 205
sympathetic nervous system 100, 145, 146, 196
synapse 205
systematic desensitization 67

T

Taub, Edward 82, 85, 86
temperature 201
temporal lobe 201, 204, 205
temporoparietal junction 205
thalamus 95, 96, 97, 201, 205
Thayer, Julian 99
The Crossing Church 208
theory of mind 205
thirst 201
Three Blessings Exercise 200
Tiemann, Dale 63, 207
transformation 10, 12, 74, 177, 193
transparency 128
trauma 6, 66, 68, 132, 146
traumatic brain injury 88, 123
tryptophan 204

U

umbrella of grace 117
uncertainty 103, 104, 105, 106, 206

United States Congress 3

V

vagal nerve tone 103, 144, 145
vagal nervous system 32, 99, 100, 101, 102, 103, 104, 107, 141, 145
vagus nerve 99, 100, 101, 102, 106
values 12, 33, 136, 143, 144, 145, 146, 152, 156, 157, 158, 159, 160, 161, 174
values-confusion 168
vasopressin 205
ventral tegmental area 198, 206
ventromedial prefrontal cortex 206
vertical integration 32, 99
virtues 33, 87
visual memories 205
voluntary movement 198

W

wakefulness 195
Warren, Kay 182
Warren, Matthew 183
Warren, Rick 128, 153
Watson, John 81
Willard, Dallas 13, 74, 151
wisdom 10, 13, 75, 88, 173, 204
Wright, N.T. 192

Y

Yancey, Phillip 42, 128
Young, William 129

Made in the USA
Lexington, KY
06 February 2016